I0144984

You Don't Look Young
For Your Age

You Don't Look Young For Your Age

Bruce Freedman

Holstein Press

2013

You Don't Look Young For Your Age
By Bruce Freedman
Holstein Press

Illustrations by Dusty Hanson & Steven K von Kampen

Copyright © 2013 by Bruce Freedman

All rights reserved. This book or any portion thereof may not be reproduced or used in any manner whatsoever without the express written permission of the publisher except for the use of brief quotations in a book review or scholarly journal.

First Printing: 2013

ISBN 978-0-9813937-0-4

This is a work of fictional non-fiction. The content is true except when it's not. Hopefully, you can tell the difference. Names have been changed to protect the easily embarrassed.

Published in Canada

For Katie, my source of inspiration

Contents

Preface

This book was seven years in the making. Not that it took so long to write it — that took just one year. The problem is what happened afterwards.

You see, after I completed it, I decided I wasn't going to look for a publisher. Publishers receive dozens of unsolicited manuscripts every day. How on earth would mine stand out? I was an ex-investment analyst writing a humour book. And while my role as an analyst in Hong Kong involved copious amounts of writing, I was not known as a writer there, and I most certainly was not known as anything in Canada, where I had just returned.

Not that I didn't want to publish my book. I wanted that very much. But if I'd learned one thing in my former vocation, it's that it's better to be recruited than to search for a job. So going hat in hand to a publisher or an agent was not my plan. I figured my time would be better spent building an audience. That would prove doubly beneficial since having a publisher doesn't mean automatic success — publishers do very little to market their authors. However, if I had an audience, not only would I have a market for my book but I'd also become more attractive to a publisher, increasing my odds of closing a deal. I'd be killing two birds with one stone.

The linchpin towards building my audience was my blog, which told my story: my story being my efforts to build an audience to listen to my story so that I could later sell them other stories — i.e. my book. No paradox here.

I blogged a couple of times of week and started doing open mikes at comedy clubs, book readings, posting videos on YouTube, submitting articles to magazines, online advertising via Google AdWords as well as old school promotional handouts — anything to gain an audience. I was having a blast. I was seeing real success too, judging from the pick up in views from non-family members.

Until late 2007. That's when three things happened: one success, one misfortune and one massive realization. Together they took the wind out of my sails.

Success

Six months after I finished the book, as part of my marketing strategy, I produced some promotional bookmarks, which contained some information about my blog, my bio and a giggle. I hired a cute girl off Craigslist to stand outside Chapters and hand them to people leaving the bookstore. It actually worked; I started seeing a meaningful increase in website views. I figured it was now time to refine my target market.

So I gave my cute girl the addresses of the top publishers in Toronto, and over the next few days joined her in front of the buildings. We offered bookmarks to all who entered from eight till eleven in the morning. (I reckoned publisher types might like to sleep in.)

On day two, the gods were with us and we were moving merchandise at a feverish pace. High on adrenaline and bookmark dust, I decided to up the ante. I entered the building and took the elevator up to HarperCollins' floor. My intention was to simply ask the receptionist to leave some bookmarks in the lunchroom. But she had not arrived and the glass front doors were locked. So I proceeded to stuff some bookmarks between the doors. And that is how I met HarperCollins' head of non-fiction.

We chatted for a while. I told him my story. He liked my story. And then he asked me if I had approached HarperCollins with my book. I told him that I had not approached anyone and

I told him why. As I explained my reasoning, he nodded and broke into a big smile. "We need more authors like you," he said. And that's when he asked me to submit a book proposal.

Misfortune

Preparing the proposal was no easy task. Book proposals follow a standard industry template and are more about the marketing strategy for the book than the book itself. I constructed mine accordingly. It dawned on me though that if I were to receive an offer from HarperCollins, I would likely have to make a quick decision. So I owed it to myself to at least try and approach some other publishers. If I got even one bite, I'd have more bargaining power with HarperCollins.

In two weeks I was headed to New York for a wedding, so I decided to spend an extra day there and attempt to connect with some top agents and publishers. But I didn't want to go the ordinary route; Instead I decided to one-up what had worked for me in Toronto. I prepared eight gift baskets, full of sketchy rejuvenating creams, Chinese herbs and adult diapers. In the bottom of the basket, I included a DVD with a video of my stand up comedy, an animated/live-action promo I had produced, a few bookmarks and of course the book proposal itself. Attached to the basket, was a handwritten card with the publisher/agent's name on it. The card read as follows:

Dear _____

You don't look young for your age.

That's right, you don't.

That's why I'm giving you these amazing anti-aging remedies and a proposal for my self-help book, You Don't Look Young For Your Age.

I stuffed the baskets into my hard-shell golf case and planned to personally deliver them when I got to New York. I arranged for a driver to shuttle me between locations. All was perfectly timed except for one small detail. Air Canada lost my luggage and only got it back to me after I returned to Toronto.

Realization

The missed opportunity in New York was disappointing, but not in itself the end of the world; I could always have booked another trip. Nor was the rejection letter from HarperCollins — which came shortly thereafter — responsible for my loss of momentum. No, the biggest factor was me. You see, while I was preparing my book proposal, I did one thing that I had not done in a long time — read my book.

During all those months of blogging and marketing, I hadn't touched my book. And when I finally opened the word document to incorporate it into the proposal, I was thrown for a loop. Simply put, I did not like it. First of all, it didn't sound like me. It was a lot angrier in tone than what I was then feeling. This probably reflected the fact that I started the book shortly after I quit my job and as my marriage was ending. Second, it felt immature. What felt clever and cute at the time now felt contrived and juvenile. Third, the writing sucked. During my year of blogging, my writing had improved dramatically. When I read what I was once certain was mind-blowing and realized it was utter crap, I was completely deflated. There was no fixing it either, not when I disliked the content too.

After numerous attempts, I put it away. A few friends suggested I self-publish it, but that held no appeal to me. They don't call self-publishing vanity-publishing for nothing; nobody buys these books. But there could be no vanity for me because I no longer liked my book. Why would I self-publish a book that I no longer liked for no one to buy?

Until now. About six months ago, I opened the file and the title invoked a new sensation in me. The title is based off the chapter of the same name. It is the very first chapter I wrote, and it was written as a tease — a playful poke in the ribs of those people around me who I thought were acting immature. I wrote it from the perspective of a cantankerous banker who worked eighty-hour weeks and sneered at artsy types, plastic surgery addicts, idealists, cynics, adults who hadn't grown up and anybody else who I thought did not 'get it.'

My grandmother was an intelligent, active woman who believed in education and that one should always seek to better oneself. She went back to high school when she was forty-nine years old and learned how to use a computer when she was eighty. My mother started law school when she was thirty-three years old and was one of the only women in her class, let alone a woman with three kids. She has a creative spirit and is always trying interesting new things: painting, tai chi and tango — you name it. I'm now happily remarried, and my wife is an actress, a writer, an opera singer, a jewelry maker, a cook, and runs a non-profit organization. I've always respected people who are curious about life and open to new experiences. I believe it keeps them young.

It occurred to me that since my return to Canada this is who I strive to be too: somebody who's not afraid to try new things, somebody who's searching for passion and zest and meaning in life. Exactly the kind of person my book title was making fun of.

It made me smile. So I reread the book. While there were definitely some issues, I realized that I'd been too hard on it. Some of the essays were actually pretty good. Others were hopeless. I killed them and edited the rest. I took a lighter approach to those chapters that spoke with a voice that was no longer my own, because even though I might cringe at the tone, I can respect the passion, humour and self-discovery that went into them. Of the original thirty-four chapters, only twenty-two survived the culling. In the spirit of thickening my now-thin book, I added nine more recent essays.

Back when I was in marketing mode, people used to ask me what my book was about and I always gave some bullshit response that it was a cross between David Sedaris and Michael Moore with a hint of *Freakonomics* thrown in. That's because there was no unifying theme. With the deletions and recent chapter additions, there's even less commonality now. The only thing I can say for certain is that this book is comprised of thirty-one hopefully humorous pieces that were written by me. Me then and me now. And while you might not agree with everything I say, rest assured that neither do I. It was all done for the smiles. And in case you're interested, I don't look young for my age, and I'm fine with that.

Acknowledgements

Thank you to all who were part of this process, be it reading and critiquing the various drafts, visiting my blog or providing otherwise invaluable input. Any errors or omissions are mine and mine alone. A special callout to my brother, Glen, who edited the most recent revision, and then told me he'd vastly improved the book. I think he took his revisions too far especially when he made himself the main character. Still, I appreciate his efforts even if I did reject most of his changes.

Back in high school, I walked out of a math test convinced I'd aced it. My friend, Walter, walked out minutes later convinced he'd aced it too. As kids do, we started talking about the test and quickly realized that we both couldn't have aced it. In fact, if one of us had indeed aced it, the other would be lucky to receive a passing grade.

Two weeks later, the teacher announced the results, saying: "On the whole, the class did rather dreadfully but I am pleased to say that we did have one perfect score. Bruce, would you please come to the front of the room and collect your exam."

While the one hundred was great, the look on Walter's face was even better. Given that Glen is almost finished writing his very first book, we'll soon discover which one of us is the Walter when it comes to writing.

A second callout to Jessica Caplan who suffered through the very first draft all those years ago — call it payback for her suggestion that I write the book in the first place.

Other supportive names: Wendy Lee Barnard; the T-Dot Writers Meetup Group; James Link; Lesley Horlick Slack; Scott Sauer; Iryna Ivanova; Jason Budovitch; Bryant Caplan; Brian Katz; my brother, David; my mother; and my nephew, Zachary, who asked me at least once every six months, "So when is your book going to be published?"

I also want to thank Dusty Hanson and Steven K von Kampen, two artists of exceptional talent who brought my stories to life. Dusty drew eight pictures including the image on the front cover several years back, while Steven illustrated the remainder only a few weeks ago.

Last, I want to thank my wife, Katie, for her love, support and fine example.

A King In A Past Life
(and an idiot in this one)

I'm on holiday in France with a group of friends and friends of friends — the reason for this distinction will become apparent in the next few paragraphs.

We are visiting the old quarter, The Church of Notre Dame. Are we going in? Apparently not, Tina has fallen to the ground, gasping for air. She can't enter the Church. Her boyfriend, Martin, helps her outside. What's wrong?

What's wrong, Martin tells us over lunch, is that Tina was a witch in a previous life. Burned at the stake by Christian priests, she can't go into the church — too many bad memories. Fortunately, she's had better experiences in her other past lives; being a duchess in one life and a queen in another are two of her favorites. In all, Tina recalls ten of her past lives.

Martin too, remembers ten past lives, the details of which are quite exciting. But what is really remarkable to me is that in eight of those lives he was hanging with Tina, five times as husband, three times as secret lover. The universe obviously has grand plans for these two soul mates. Let's hope Martin remembers to put the toilet seat down.

Noting that my friends at the table do not seem at all surprised by Martin's comments, I decide to tread lightly and carefully admit some skepticism.

Believe it or not, Martin, who is not royalty in this life, is surprised by my skepticism and takes the offensive, "Look, you're entitled to your view, but have you done any research? You should do some research before being so quick to judge. You've only got nine hundred million people in the world who believe in reincarnation. It's a belief system that's been around for thousands of years. There are countless books on the subject and I personally have distinct memories of past lives. Are you going to deny that?"

I tell him that I'll 'do the research' in one my future lives. Besides, if there really was compelling proof of reincarnation, wouldn't it have found a better way to capture my attention than being printed in magazines made of recycled paper?

But that isn't true. I can't wait until my next life to prove him wrong. When I return to my hotel room that night, I decide to do some research. Now, I'll never be able to prove reincarnation is impossible, so I instead decide to tackle his numbers. I ask myself, if Tina and Martin were reincarnated ten times, then it's only fair to assume that everybody else was reincarnated ten times too, right? Otherwise, we'd have to argue that they were a special case, some kind of super soul, and that would be a stretch even though they are both yoga instructors.

I do the math. In order for each person alive on this planet today to have been reincarnated ten times, there must have been seventy billion human lives lived since the dawn of man.

Otherwise, we wouldn't have enough meat-containers to hold all these souls.

Is it possible? I scour the internet and there is a surprisingly large amount of articles to be found on this subject, with the consensus thinking being one hundred billion human beings have lived on this planet since Homo sapiens first appeared fifty thousand years ago.

But we've still got a problem. There may have been a hundred billion lives lived, but how do we explain the fact that mankind originated from rather limited numbers. Whether you believe in Adam and Eve, or a particularly smart monkey named Lucy, it's indisputable that the population of those first Homo sapiens was dramatically smaller than it is today.

So where did all the souls come from to fill the seven billion human bodies that are walking and breathing today, let alone the hundred billion across history? Some giant bowl?

The next morning over a breakfast of bacon and eggs, I share my thoughts with Martin.

He responds, "You're forgetting the fact that not every soul in a human body today necessarily came from a human body in its previous life. There are many theories as to reincarnation; some Buddhists for instance see the human vessel as the apex of the process. A soul is reborn many times, and it spends countless lifetimes in the lower forms of life, such as insects. Only as it spiritually advances, is it rewarded by being reborn as a higher life form. When you include all forms of animal life you'll see that there are more than enough potential souls to supply the human bodies out there."

I push my plate away.

But this leaves me with another question, one that I contemplate after the trip. There are many animals on planet Earth, which means there are many souls. With each one of these souls competing for human bodies what are the odds that a soul will be reborn into a human body, not once, not twice, but ten times?

To answer this, we need to get a feel for just how many animals there are. By most estimates, there are easily one million species. And that's just recorded species. A recent study published by *PLOS Biology* rather precisely estimates that there are 7.77 million species of animals (give or take 958,000).

Now we've got roughly seven billion human beings. But what is the total population of all the other species? Google provides little help here.

Cats? Dogs? Cows? Certainly over a billion each, I would imagine.

What about insects? According to the Harvard scientist, E.O Wilson, there are more than a hundred trillion ants in the world. That's sixteen thousand ants for every person. While I am sure there are many skeptics wondering how one can even count ants, I can personally testify that at least one billion of those ants populated my very first apartment.

And what about fish? Seventy percent the earth is covered by water, so there's a lot of seafood to be counted. I had fifteen shrimps with fried rice for dinner just last night; that's a lot of souls in one helping.

The bottom line is that there are tens of thousands (if not millions) of animal souls for every human soul, each and every one of them competing for a better body after they die.

So let me ask the believers: over the course of human history, what are the odds that you — a cow, a shrimp or an alligator — are promoted to the human body not once, not twice, but ten times? And to be royalty as well?

I don't know the answer to that, but if you still maintain that you were royalty in a past life, you need to accept it was probably as a queen bee, a king prawn or an emperor penguin.

Oh and Martin and Tina? Putting the universe's grand plans aside, they broke up less than a year after the trip.

You Can't Drive Anymore

In what turned out to the last boys' trip before we met our wives, two friends and I went on a ten-day tour of New Zealand. Our plan was to have no plan. We would rent a car and drive across the South Island — from Christchurch to Queenstown — each of us taking a turn at the wheel. The landscape was spectacular, though we were disappointed that we saw no hobbits.

The back seat was stuffed with luggage and the three of us were always arguing as to who would sit in front. Except when I was driving. When it was my turn at the wheel, my friends would tense up and argue about who got to sit in the back. They said I wasn't a particularly good driver. I laughed it off, thinking they were just teasing me.

On the fourth day, we were in the hilly terrain surrounding Mount Cook — where they filmed *Vertical Limit*. I was at the wheel and navigating a particularly steep and winding road. There were no barriers along the edge of the slope to protect us from what would be certain death. My friends hollered and screamed on every curve. I thought they were just having fun, until we stopped for lunch. They turned to me and said something to this effect: "We're sorry, Bruce. We're not teasing you. This is not a joke. We don't want to make you feel bad. But the simple truth is, you can't drive anymore. We're afraid for our lives when you're behind the wheel."

Unlike most men, I've never loved to drive. There must be something wrong with my brain — something to do with spatial relationships — because I'm never quite sure where the edges of my car are. Either that or it's the fear of a collision that was instilled in me as a child by my loving but overprotective parents.

My fear of automobiles is just the tip of the iceberg. My parents always believed it was good to expect the worst. Whether it was driving my bicycle on the sidewalk or ensuring that nobody slipped drugs into my hamburger at lunch, there was so much danger to be avoided. I think many of the unconventional choices I've made in my life were attempts to conquer these fears. No matter how much I've hidden it on the surface though, fear has always been a part of me.

In my mid-twenties, I finally succumbed to my childhood fantasy of driving a motorcycle — or perhaps more accurately: my childhood fantasy of being the kind of guy that would drive a motorcycle. My first — and last — bike was a 250cc Honda Shadow. If I had gotten a vehicle with an engine any smaller, I could have also used it to cut my lawn. My friends in Hong Kong gave me a lot of grief when they saw me on my bike. Even the pizza deliverymen were driving bigger bikes than me. I did not care. My small bike was a calculated decision. I prudently decided to gain valuable experience on a smaller bike before upgrading to a more powerful engine. That never happened. I probably drove the bike no more than a dozen times before I gave up the hobby altogether. The frightening statistic that most motorcycle accidents are caused by the negligence of others eventually overwhelmed me. I also couldn't shake the less reasonable fear that the front wheel of my bike might suddenly disengage while I was cruising on the highway.

When I moved back to Canada, as a new resident in Ontario, I was required to take the G2 road test. The fact that I had fifteen years of driving experience overseas was irrelevant as far as the government was concerned. Given my driving skills, this was probably a good thing.

To pass, you must make less than thirty-two errors. To fail, you must make more than thirty-two errors. I made thirty-two errors exactly, which left my fate to the examiner's discretion. Before writing 'pass' on the page, he chastised me for a sloppy left turn — my first turn out of the gates. I had turned left but did not enter the left-most lane. He also claimed I cut off a car doing a right-hand turn. I begged to differ. I did not recall seeing that car. I did not voice that thought to him.

Back in the past where I was a teenager, my brother and I were arguing with our parents one winter evening. We were both new drivers and our parents had just forbidden us to drive the family car "when it rains, snows or after dark."

"But Mom … Dad?" I said. "Is this a good idea for our mental development? We're going to have to drive in rain or snow or the dark, one day. What kind of drivers will we be when we're adults if we have a fear of these natural phenomena? And what will this do to our confidence and self image?" I probably didn't phrase my argument quite this well, but that's how I remember it.

My mother praised me for my logic and critical reasoning. Then she said, "I'm not worried about your driving. It's everybody else's driving that concerns me. There are a lot of crazies on the road. Let's worry about your future later. My job is to keep you alive now."

Life After JDate

When I moved to Toronto, divorced and delighted, I initially stayed with my brother's family. It was wonderful. I got to spend some quality time with my nephews. I enjoyed playing the caring uncle. But it wasn't enough. After a few weeks, I realized I needed to get out. I needed to meet grownups, people who would agree that six hours of *Guitar Hero* is excessive. And preferably people with long legs, flaming red hair and tattoos on the smalls of their backs.

I'd heard about *Lavalife* and *Matchmaker* and this internet dating phenomenon, but I'd never been on any of the websites. I met my future ex-wife back when internet dating was still a novelty. I'd been told that internet dating was no longer an embarrassment. Sure there were disaster stories, but there were success stories too. And one of my closest friends married the woman he met on *JDate*, an internet dating site that caters to

Jews. It seemed like a lot of harmless fun to me.

Now, I'm not a particularly good Jew. I'd dated only one Jewish woman in my life. So I figured that if I'm going to try internet dating, I owed it to my mother to do it through *JDate*. So I set up an account, uploaded a couple of pictures of myself, and what happens? You know that old episode of *The Twilight Zone* where an entire town wakes up to discover they've lost a week of their lives because some aliens had kidnapped them and placed them in suspended animation?

That's what *JDate* did to me.

You may as well have removed that week from my life, because I can barely remember it. All I know is that during this period, I did not work, I did not go to the gym and I did not leave the house. I did not even go on any actual dates. I just sat in front of my computer reading Jewish women's profiles, responding to emails and eating too much cereal.

Have you ever played a video game for the first time against a friend who's been playing it for weeks? You know that moment where the game has just begun — and you're trying to figure out which button does what — and suddenly your friend comes running up behind you and blows you up with a rocket launcher? You're pleading for a grace period to learn how the controls work but every time you're reborn, he immediately shoots you. That's what *JDate* is like for the uninitiated. Within seconds of activating my profile, I was attacked. Instant messages were popping up like Bouncing Bettys. By the end of the first minute, I'd received three 'flirts' and been 'hot-listed' twice. I was overwhelmed with the attention.

I received over fifty emails in that first week. I didn't actually have time to meet any of the authors; I was too busy writing back. I had not yet learned the appropriate etiquette so I was responding to all inquiries — and I do mean all. I exchanged flirty email banter with everyone from a 54-year-old divorcee with two 17-year-old twins to a 290-pound student who was trying to decide her major. I just didn't know how to say no.

By week two, I had learned that I didn't need to know how to say 'no' — not when I could simply ignore the email. This freed up some time for me to actually go on dates.

One thing I can safely say I have learned from those first few dates is that everybody has at least one good photo. Another thing I learned is this is usually the photo that is shown on *JDate*. Some of these photos can be a bit dated. I learned this the hard way, when I sipped coffee one afternoon with a 65-year-old retiree. She had flown all the way from Iowa for the date. I really should have said no, but she looked so cute in the photo; I had not noticed the horse and buggy in the background.

My initial dating experiences were also tarnished because it took me some time to learn that there was a completely different language used among online daters. For instance, in the world of *JDate* there is no word for 'fat.' In each member's profile, there is a scroll-down menu with several possible descriptions for body-type, none of which actually reads 'fat.' Once you understand this reality, and have taken the time to learn the appropriate *JDate* diction, then you will do just fine. My tastes gravitated towards women who had selected 'lean/slender,' 'athletic/fit' or 'firm & toned.' Even then, I had some surprises. 'Athletic/fit' for the typical Jewish girl means she wears Lululemon when she's shopping.

There were also distinct rules of engagement, specific to internet dating. One lesson I quickly caught onto is that you had better want to be a father. When filling in the profile, I was asked if I planned on having children? I mistakenly chose 'maybe.' I learned afterwards that this was the wrong answer. One aspiring mom told me she could not go out with me unless I was more certain. I vehemently defended my 'maybe,' because how could I 'plan' to have children if I had not yet met the right woman. I even offered to leave my condoms at home on our first date, to prove my sincerity about impregnating her.

I finally started to get the hang of it. And while my dating life improved, I never came close to meeting that next love of my life. These so-called dates felt like job interviews. And while I got pretty good at expressing the top three reasons I'd make a good father or turning my weaknesses into strengths, there was never any real connection. It just wasn't fun.

Certainly not as much as fun as simply exploring the website. The truth is, emailing all those potential mates was far more exciting than actually meeting them. The possibilities were exhilarating, the reality less so. What these sites were really offering was the dream. And sometimes the only way to keep the dream alive is to keep your eyes closed.

One night while I was sleeping, I had a dream of a different sort. In my nightmare, I saw dozens of angry female faces floating over my still and silent body. Which brings me to instant messaging, the bane of any new user's existence. Picture this: you're minding your own business, trying to think of something clever to say in your next email, when suddenly out of nowhere, a little box floats across the computer screen. Inside the box is a picture of a woman, say FLOWER4U123, with an attached flashing caption:

> *"FLOWER4U123 would like to instant message you. Do you accept?"*

You've got two choices: 'yes' or 'no.' If you choose nothing the box eventually will go away, but it takes a very long time. I always felt my pulse racing when that box appeared. I never had the heart to click 'no' because then the sender would receive an automatic message, saying that I refused her instant message. So I did nothing. The worst part about it was that the picture in the box was usually a cropped close-up of the smiling woman's face. So it looked like some disembodied, cackling head floating on my screen.

Sometimes, I'd open up another window to get away but the head actually followed me to the next page. On one particularly stormy night, I had three heads floating across my screen. It was like something out of *The Texas Chainsaw Massacre*. I ran from the room.

About a month after I started using *JDate*, I had a rude awakening. I'd received emails from over fifty women in that first week alone but after that initial flood of interest for the new boy in town, the excitement wore off. No new emails came my way. I'd log onto the site looking for new faces, trying to stir up some interest, but it was no use. I now recognized many members, and they recognized me. We'd been down this road before. For a while, I kept emailing my initial 'relationships' to keep the dream alive. But it wasn't the same. I'd lost them: my angels, my flock, my girls.

In the beginning, I felt invincible, omnipotent, like I was the king of the world. The dates may have been uneventful, but the potential was always there. But now even that feeling was gone. *JDate* left me broken, a shadow of my former self. Perhaps it was truly time for me to move on.

Still, I was grateful for the experience. Internet dating may have been a tease, but in giving me that taste of celebrity, it gave me a glimpse of the past, memories of greatness, memories I did not even know I had forgotten: birthday parties as a child, catching that fly ball in the bottom of the ninth and being kissed by a first love. And while I recognized that those golden years were gone forever, I was still left with some hope. There was life after *JDate* after all. For starters, there was *Lavalife*, *Matchmaker* and of course *Plentyoffish* too.

The Fifth 'C' Of Buying An Engagement Ring

So I'm shopping for an engagement ring for my future ex-wife. I already have a pretty good idea in terms of what I want. Not that I'm so intuitive about women or anything like that. No, she had told me a year earlier exactly what she wanted if she were ever to get married, hint, hint. And like a good boyfriend, I had written it down.

I'm lucky. I'm sitting in a friend's office. He works in the family business, one of the largest diamond wholesalers in Asia. He normally deals with ridiculously wealthy customers so I'm fortunate that he's doing me this favour. I know I'm not going to get ripped off.

I quickly learn that there is a whole different language when it comes to buying an engagement ring. You've got four Cs to be aware of: clarity, color, cut and carat.

- *'Clarity' refers to the purity of the diamond. Apparently, there are defects inside a diamond. I say 'apparently' because most of these flaws can only be seen with the help of a microscope or a magnifying glass. Not even your girlfriend's bionic vision, which can spot a poorly washed plate from the other side of the kitchen, could detect most defects.*

- *'Color' measures the extent of discoloring in a white diamond. There are twenty-three different grades of white, with 'D' (colorless) being the most valuable and 'Z' (light yellow) the least desirable. I've always been a bit slow when it comes to languages. I only mastered my ABCs in grade three. Perhaps that's why my eyes could detect no difference between D, E, F and G.*

- *'Cut' measures craftsmanship, taking into account symmetry, cut and polish. The better the cut, the better the refraction of light and the more brilliant the end result. There is no grading system for this very important C so most shoppers pay little heed to it. Instead, they obsess about clarity and color where without a grading system, they would not be able to tell the difference.*

- *'Carat' refers to the size of the diamond. Bigger is always better. Unfortunately, bigger is also more expensive. Too bad our women don't like their diamonds the way they like their dress size.*

I'm sitting there getting very confused by all this new terminology. I want to get my girl what she asked for, because anything less means I don't love her, right? Unfortunately, he does not have her exact specifications in stock. I have to make some decisions on my own. I'm not a stupid man. I err towards the more expensive. Only the best for my girl.

It never even occurs to me to get her anything other than a real diamond, although there are alternatives. There are simulated diamonds, like Cubic Zirconia, which simply look like natural diamonds. And there are manufactured diamonds that have an identical chemical composition. Both of these substitutes are significantly cheaper than natural diamonds. That is, until you factor in the emotional cost of trying to convince your fiancé that you're not a penny-pinching jackass.

It's understandable why most women would not want a simulated diamond. It is quite easy to tell it apart from natural diamond. Cubic Zirconia, for instance, is very heavy. A one-carat real diamond weighs roughly the same as two toothpicks. A Cubic Zirconia stone of similar size would weigh the backbreaking equivalent of three and a half toothpicks.

Cubic Zirconia is also not as durable as real diamond. Sure, it can scratch glass and steel and is harder than just about any other natural gem. But it's not as strong as the real deal. This is a major roadblock to greater acceptance. After all, women's engagement rings undergo so much duress.

Cubic Zirconia is also distinguishable from natural diamond in that it is unusually flawless and perfect in color. It's just too good to be true. No, we definitely don't want to buy Cubic Zirconia. Let's just leave it for the losers who watch *The Home Shopping Network*.

But what about manufactured diamonds? Can we give a manufactured diamond engagement ring to our women? Also called 'synthetic' or 'artificial,' manufactured diamonds are produced in a factory. They are atomically equivalent to real diamonds. In other words, they don't just look the same — they are the same. There is no disagreement on this fact within the diamond industry. Even the head of the well-respected Gemological Institute of America (GIA) has stated that they have all the "same optical, physical and chemical properties of a natural diamond." And unlike blood diamonds, nobody dies to make them.

Most manufactured diamonds come in fancy colors like blue, pink or green, which has limited their opportunity in the mass market, where white engagement rings are the norm. Diamond manufacturers could make white stones just as easily, but fancy colors enjoy a significant price premium, so manufacturers have targeted this more lucrative market first. Consumer acceptance is still surprisingly slow. Manufactured colored diamonds sell for less than a third the price of the natural mined ones.

The public may be wary, but commercial enterprises know a good thing when they see it. They know that a manufactured diamond is no different than the 'real' thing. That's why corporations that use diamond in the industrial process mainly buy manufactured stones. In fact, industrial demand is so strong that there are three carats of diamond manufactured for every carat of diamond that is mined.

Karl Marx wrote in his book *Capital*, "If we could succeed, at a small expenditure of labor, in converting carbon into diamonds, their value might fall below that of bricks." Well, the alchemists have succeeded. Industry is pleased with this development but the man-on-the street is clueless. Marx neglected to consider the power of marketing, as well as the ability of the consumer to be duped.

There appears to be a war of words, or better yet, semantics, going on between the various industry players. For instance, in 2006, GIA announced that it would begin issuing manufactured diamond grading reports. This pleased the manufacturers, until they discovered that GIA would use the word 'synthetic' to describe manufactured diamonds rather than their preference for 'man-made.' GIA also stated its labs would laser-inscribe the word 'synthetic' on the girdle of every manufactured diamond it grades. And if this weren't humiliating enough, GIA's synthetic diamond reports would be printed on distinctive yellow paper.

So, despite its lack of flaws and perfect coloring, the typical woman does not want a Cubic Zirconia ring because it weighs too many toothpicks and can be broken with extraordinary force. Nor does she desire a manufactured diamond, even though it's atomically identical to a natural stone. What she does desire is a natural diamond ring. Perhaps it's because 'diamonds are forever?' Diamonds may well be forever, but De Beers only introduced that very successful marketing slogan in 1947. Before then, the gems of choice for an engagement ring were opals, rubies and sapphires.

And these natural diamonds, which you're told are a great investment, will lose you money the moment you walk out of the store. Just try selling your ring back to a retailer. Even on *eBay*, which has made it so easy for the public to monetize their unwanted ashtrays and garden gnomes, diamonds are one product where amateur vendors are at a significant disadvantage.

Still, if you were to present all these facts to your fiancé, and try to convince her to accept a simulated diamond, a manufactured diamond or even some other natural gem, chances are her eyes would narrow, her voice would harden and she would calmly state that she requires the real deal. Perhaps that's what a diamond ring is really about. There is nothing sensible about a diamond. Rather, it's tangible proof that you are willing to put your love for another human being above your own beliefs. You are putting her wishes above your own. In other words, you are truly ready to completely surrender yourself to the conciliations inherent in a healthy marriage. Which brings us to the fifth 'C' of the process: 'compromise.' Or is it 'capitulation?'

I Deserve Nice Things
(because I'm worth it)

Last night I cooked myself a proper dinner, using my shiny new stainless steel pots and professional chef's knives. It was the first time I've cooked since my divorce two months ago. It felt great — like I was a civilized person. It's been quite the year. Exactly twelve months ago, I separated from my wife. I've stayed in hotels, serviced apartments, friend's spare bedrooms, and most recently my brother's house. The idea of cooking for myself has never been more appealing.

If I'm going to do something, then I'm going to do it right. So when I needed to buy pots and knives, I spoke to my sister-in-law. She knows where to get the good stuff. And she told me to go to Williams-Sonoma.

For those of you who don't know the store, according to its

website, Williams-Sonoma was established in 1956 with the goal of 'bringing the best French kitchenware to home cooks in America.' Now I'm no miser. I may shop more than occasionally at IKEA but I know better than to buy my cookware from them. At the same time, I'm no spendthrift either. I don't need the best stuff. I don't want the best stuff. I simply want the best stuff that someone of my caliber would appreciate.

So I'm never going to buy that two hundred dollar bottle of wine; it would be wasted on my taste buds. And I wasn't about to spend a fortune buying 'the best French kitchenware.' I had the feeling that Williams-Sonoma was not going to be interested in my business. I had no intention of going there.

Still, a few weeks ago, I was walking through a mall, and saw the store sign. I couldn't resist popping in. Within seconds of entering the store, I knew I'd made a mistake. The place was overflowing with members of the preternaturally young Botox club. I started eyeballing the prices in the pots and pans section. The cheapest set was over five hundred dollars and some sets were over a thousand dollars. I turned to leave but it was too late. A handsome, gray-haired woman in her fifties was already approaching me, and I was caught in her vise-like stare.

'Elizabeth' reminded me of Professor McGonagall of the Harry Potter movies. She was not a tall woman but had an air of command. Her lips said 'Can I help you' but her eyes said, 'You are mine.' I cursed myself for wearing my Ralph Lauren long, wool overcoat, the one that makes me look like a successful businessman, instead of a struggling writer. I was in big trouble.

Elizabeth knew her stuff. This was no smarmy sales-person. She was knowledgeable and wise in a mother-earth kind of way. She spoke of the vast considerations when buying pots and pans: heat conductivity, safety and the Teflon/stainless-steel debate. I felt my free will slipping away.

Have you ever been in the presence of a lawyer who charges five hundred dollars an hour, and doesn't know when to shut up?

You have butterflies in your belly because you know every syllable she utters is going to cost you more money. That's how I felt with Elizabeth. Every word she uttered was valuable — knowledge accrued over her long life. I wanted her to stop talking. Of course I would buy something. I owed her for her time.

Luckily, at that precise instant, a baby started shrieking. The high frequency vibrations brought me out of her spell, and during that window of lucidity, I thanked her for her time, and told her that I would 'think about it.' She mercifully granted my leave and I limped off to another part of the store. I did not want her to see me leave. I belonged there, yes, I did.

But the story does not end there. I entered the knives

section. I was examining the knife display, or should I say, the prices. A question popped into my head. There was a stock girl doing inventory nearby — young and harmless looking — so I felt safe talking to her. I instantly regretted it when she gave me her answer:

"I'm sorry, I don't know a whole lot about the knives, but let me get our resident expert."

She walked away and within seconds returned with whom else but Elizabeth. Now I was truly lost. I put up no resistance and immediately chose the cheapest set she had, three knives plus a knife sharpener for three hundred dollars. How many tomatoes would I have to cut to justify spending this much? I tried to make myself feel better by reminding myself of how hard I've worked in my life. Why shouldn't I cut with the best? I was worth it!

But it turned out the gods were smiling on me this day. Because as I dejectedly stood by the cash register waiting for my box, the stock girl returned and said she could not find any unopened packages. "But I know we have two sets," Elizabeth said.

"Not a problem," I graciously said. "I have a lot of shopping to do and will be in the mall for the next hour. Why don't you call me when you can find them and I'll just pop back and pick them up."

I tried not to break into a dance as I exited the store. Elizabeth's magic over me was so strong, that in normal circumstances, I might not have been able to refuse her phone call. Except here, I had an ace up my sleeve. Her magic was strong, but my wireless provider was weak. I never got good reception in this particular mall, so I would not have to do battle again.

Ultimately, I did buy two knives — a Chef's knife and a Santoku — and a whole set of pots at one of my favorite stores,

Linens and Things. They cost me three hundred bucks. Perfect. I did not escape scot-free though because the sales person did still convince me to buy the knife sharpener — to better enjoy my knives — for an additional fifty dollars. It still sits unopened in the drawer. And whether I use it or not, the bottom line is, I deserve it. Because I'm worth it.

You Don't Look Young For Your Age

My friends think they look young — but they don't. They don't look young. They don't look young at all. In fact, they look like shit. Jim is almost completely bald and has dark spots the size of tea bags under his forty-year-old eyes. And Martin? Martin reminds me of Nicholas Cage. He's in great shape and still prowls the nightclubs. But does he think clubbers aren't going to notice those puffy jowls and receding hairline? No, my guy friends don't look so young — not at all.

And the females? Looking at them reminds me of my teenage years. Not because they look young, but because they look the way my friends' moms looked when I was in high school. They have crow's feet, lopsided bottoms and their chests are freckled from too much sun over their long lives. One of them even has a fourteen-year-old daughter, for Christ's sake!

The simple reality is that none of my friends look young for their age. I'm not saying they look old. They simply look their age. This all makes me very sad. Because it occurs to me, if they don't look so young, then maybe I don't look so young either. It can't be true. I look young for my age, right? Sure, I do. None of my friends do, but I do.

I cannot think of many women who haven't at some point asked me how old they look. I always — always — subtract four years from my real guess. And if she's over forty, I subtract eight years. Their old eyes shimmer with pleasure at my response.

Contrary to popular belief, plastic surgery or Botox does not help. At best, it might take a few years off, but you can never achieve any meaningful impact. Everyone knows that instead of looking like a sixty-year-old with wrinkles, you look like a sixty-year-old without wrinkles. Something always looks unnatural.

And what's with this 'forty is the new thirty' bullshit? Forty may be the new thirty, but I guarantee you one thing: you're still going to be hanging out with other miserable forty-year-olds. That's because the thirty-year-olds will be sticking to their own age bracket. Is that because thirty is now the new twenty?

A few friends have suggested I start coloring my hair. I still have a good head of hair but it's gray around the temples. I hate it and wish it were brown. But I've resisted dying it, because, deep down, I know it's a battle I cannot win. I'm not saying that I don't want to look good and take care of myself. It's more that once you begin this process, where does it end? You're up against Mother Nature, and she always wins. I'd rather try to come to terms with my aging, because it's simply a fact of life. It's not easy, but at least I look younger than my friends.

My Dream Girl

I recently ended things with my dream girl. I kept it going longer than I should have, hoping that she was 'the one.' But in the end, I accepted there was no future. In a healthy relationship, you should both grow, basking in each other's radiance. It can't be a one-way street. But with her it was. I'm not saying there was anything wrong with her. 'Nikki' was my perfect woman, but I was just another guy as far as she was concerned.

I met Nikki at the Starbucks across from my condo. I was drinking a coffee and puttering away on my laptop. Nikki noticed me before I noticed her — or should I say, she noticed my laptop. She approached me and said, "I'm thinking of getting a MacBook too, do you like it?"

I looked up. My dream girl, standing right in front of me. She was five foot six inches tall with bright green eyes, accentuated by too much eyeliner. She looked like a porcelain doll, her perfect Japanese Anime features made even more attractive by slightly crooked, white teeth. Her rainbow-colored hair was cut in the angular style of Milla Jovovich in *The Fifth Element* — Ruby Rush R68 by L'Oreal with a dash of Platinum Crystal 120, perhaps? Her naturally pale skin — while freckled and sunburned — still retained much of the effervescent quality of her youth; she was at least a year away from exhibiting the effects of too much sun exposure. She was wearing tight cropped white pants and a green V-neck sweater — the edge of a tattoo just visible in the gap between sweater and pants.

She was so wrong for me. But oh … she was so right.

I answered her enthusiastically, gushing on the greatness of the Mac. By the time I was finished, Bill Gates would have been a believer. But I had little else to say to her. As the last words dribbled out, she turned away, collected her Venti Soy Milk Latte, and clip-clopped away to the streetcar.

The second time I saw her was two days later. I was sitting in my usual spot, the comfy chair near the window. I noticed her just as she was leaving. I looked out the window and watched her walk away, her stiletto heels preventing her from taking anything but the smallest steps. I felt something in my chest ache. I was twitterpated — without a doubt. I noted the time on my phone: 8:25 a.m. And the other day? It had been around the same time. A plan began to emerge.

It's hard to believe given the magnitude of my initial attraction that I feel absolutely nothing for her right now. My feelings didn't disappear overnight. In the last few weeks, there's been a void growing between us — no real communication. We've drifted apart. When I woke up this morning, it finally hit me that it was truly over. She means nothing to me now.

But three months ago, it was fresh and alive. Following that second serendipitous sighting, I knew I had to see her again. So the very next day, I timed my Starbucks visit with her arrival. I put on my writer's outfit — sweater vest with collared shirt and dark jeans, freshly laundered. I took the time to shave, and messed up my hair just right. I plopped myself down in my armchair fifteen minutes prior to her arrival.

I didn't get much work done, lifting my eyes more frequently than normal, to see if she had arrived. The truth is, I wasn't even really trying to work. I kept myself busy by changing the font in my word document, from Times New Roman to Arial and back again.

And then she arrived. Hot. Hot. Hot. This time though, another woman, slim and attractive, accompanied her. I looked up expectantly. But Nikki wouldn't acknowledge my existence.

She stood not three feet from me, but never once looked at me. Did she not want to talk about MacBooks anymore?

Over the next few weeks, I saw her perhaps a dozen times, often with that same woman. I did not get even one glance. I tried switching seats, thinking perhaps this was the problem. But it never worked; this woman had an anti-me antenna, which told her where not to look.

But two can play at that game. I fought fire with fire and went on strike, withholding my glances and keeping my eyes on my laptop. I typed furiously whenever she entered the coffee shop. I imagined her deeply regretting her mistake as she admired my productivity. But whenever I did steal a glance — because I could never totally ignore her — she was looking somewhere else.

Fortunately, I'm not just some naive schoolboy. There's been pain in my life and that pain has given me the experience to know when I need to break from unhealthy patterns. I'm not exactly sure when it happened but last night it occurred to me that I hadn't seen or thought of her in weeks. My morning coffees no longer coincided with her schedule — not that I was avoiding her, I'd just forgotten she existed. We finally had something in common. But it was now too late for us. You see, I've moved on. I've met a new dream girl, with long curly hair — Flaming Red R75 — at The Second Cup.

Expensive Accommodation Indeed

If there is one thing I have learned in life, it is that you should never stay at a friend or relative's place when you are on holiday. Sure, your financial expenditure might be low, but your psychological expenditure will be high.

In particular, you should never do this if you have other friends in the same city that you plan to see. Because these friends never seem to be that friendly with the friend you are staying with. Sure, they might pop over and chitchat with your host when you are in town, but they never, ever hang out with each other after you leave.

This makes things difficult when you are visiting town for a short period of time. You are now in a lose-lose situation. When you hang out with your other pals, you feel guilty. Like you are a bad guest taking advantage of your hosts.

But you also feel bad when you spend too much time with your hosts. Because those other buddies always seem to be more fun than the friends you are staying with. It is their more interesting lives, by the way, that practically guarantees that their residences will not be as nice as the place you are staying. Which explains why you're not staying with them. It's a catch-22.

So you run yourself ragged the entire holiday, trying to spend quality time with your hosts while also partying with your other friends. You gain ten pounds because you don't have the time to work out, and you feel compelled each night to eat dinner with your hosts, before grabbing a second, better dinner with your fun friends.

And the amount of fun you have on a holiday is inversely correlated to the number of children your host has. In fact, you would be absolutely mad to stay with a friend with children, unless you never plan to leave the house. Here you are, expecting to sample the city's finest restaurants, but you're stuck eating chicken nuggets at six o'clock in the evening and hearing about Andrew's day at school. You want to see a play on Broadway? No can do, but Natalie is playing one of the orphans in *Annie*, would you like to go? So you play along, before slinking off at ten o'clock just as your hosts are going to sleep. You party till dawn with your other friends, but still force yourself out of bed at eight in the morning so you can have breakfast with the family. You want to spend quality time with everybody, you see. Your hosts though make comments like, "Once you have kids, you'll see there's more to life than partying" or "Don't you get tired of the party lifestyle?" Funny, that they should say that, since they are the ones with the bags under their eyes.

And while you will probably ignore my advice because you're cheap, I warn you, it's never as cheap as you hoped. Sure, you save on the hotel bill. But you will inevitably take your hosts out for an expensive dinner. You'll bring them flowers, bottles of wine, and gifts for the kids. And there are other costs to consider. Instead of sleeping on a soft king-sized bed and enjoying room service, you'll find yourself on a lumpy futon and tiptoeing around the house at night so as not to wake the children. You'll set the table at dinner and help with the dishes. You'll wipe your face with toilet paper and put used floss in your pocket given the lack of towels and garbage receptacles in the guest bathroom.

The most painful outlay, though, is your contractual obligation to compliment every aspect of their lives, from their silverware to their six packs:

➪ *"Mmm mmm, great dinner, delicious."*

⇨ *"So, what do you think the stock market's going to do next year? Uh-huh … uh-huh … yeah, yeah."*

⇨ *"Yeah, he's really cute. He's going to be one handsome devil when he gets older."*

⇨ *"Yeah, I can tell. Your working out is really paying off!"*

Come to think of it, your friends should be paying you to stay there. Not just because of all the gifts you've given them, which pretty much equals what you would have spent on a hotel. And not because of the non-stop ego boosting and emotional support that you provide. But because they then get to insult you after you leave, telling everyone who will listen how messy you were and how you need to grow up.

Mrs. Freedman Will Have To Wait

When it comes to love, I have a fear. It's not a fear of being alone, quite the opposite. I'm scared of being in a relationship. It's not because I'm ruined or sad or damaged from my divorce. No, something happened recently that changed me. Something so profound that I realized I need to be alone. I cannot be in a relationship right now. Not if I want to truly control my life, my destiny, my free will. You see a few weeks ago I met with a psychic, and her predictions have turned my blood cold.

I'm not normally the superstitious type. Yes, I grew up on science fiction and fantasy but once I entered the real world, society required I put those books away. And just like any respectable member of society, the moment someone speaks of spirits, energy or psychic powers, I tend to dismiss them as a flake. That said, I don't go out of my way to step on any sidewalk cracks.

During the Toronto Film Festival, the streets were so crowded, one could barely see the sidewalks, let alone the cracks on them. I wandered through Yorkville with a friend one fine evening.

We found ourselves standing next to a psychic. She had set up a card table with two chairs right outside an ice cream shop. I've never been to a psychic. I would never go to a psychic. Especially a psychic who could not afford an office.

But we were having a good time. We started to talk to the 'customer' who was just leaving. He raved about her. He'd been seeing her for ten years.

"This card table's been here for ten years?" I thought but did not say.

Still for only ten dollars, she would read my fortune. Lack of office notwithstanding, I decided to go for it. Michael Landon didn't have an office in *Highway to Heaven*, and it didn't stop him from saving humanity. So why not give her a chance? I sat down. She asked for my hand. I started to give it to her, but then I suddenly pulled it back.

"Wait a minute," I said. "I need to understand this better. Just what exactly will I be getting for ten dollars?"

"I will tell you your past, your present and your future." She reached for my hand.

"Hang on for a second," I said, holding my hand close to my chest. "I don't need to know about my past or my present. I'm already familiar with it. I don't want you wasting your power on stuff I already know. Let's just get to the meat of it."

"OK, OK," she said. Her hand reached out for mine.

But then I suddenly realized that perhaps I didn't want to know the future. I'm not a superstitious type, but why risk it? I asked her, "But what if you read my fortune and you see something terrible about my life? I don't know if I really want to hear it."

"Do not worry. I will not tell you bad things," she said. Her hand twitched.

"But wait a minute. I don't want you to lie to me," I said.

"I won't lie to you."

"But I still don't know that I want to know."

"Don't worry so much. Besides the future is not set in stone."

"It's not set in stone? I can change it? Really?"

"Really." She looked at me. I grudgingly gave her my hand. She gripped it firmly and started to read. She got off to a shaky start and an even shakier finish.

"You're married." She declared.

"No I'm not!" I blurted out. "I'm divorced."

She stared at me and carefully enunciated. "I was not finished. You are going to be married. Again. Next year."

Wow, this woman was good. She went on. In a nutshell:

- *I'm going to get married next year.*

- *We will have two kids.*

- *I will make money in real estate. I should buy a condo.*

- *I will be very successful. I will work very hard for the next three years and then the money will flow in. In ten years time, life will be very easy.*

- *I will have good health and live a long life. Oh, and die when I'm eighty-eight.*

"Wait a minute!" I screamed. "What do you mean die at eighty-eight? You said a few minutes ago that I could change the future. You said it's flexible! Are you telling me that I am 100 percent going to die when I'm eighty-eight?"

"Yes," she said. "It says so right here. Eighty-eight." She pushed her finger hard into my palm. Why was she smiling?

I felt sick to my stomach. My future was set in stone after all. My friend couldn't understand why I was so bothered; Eighty-eight is a pretty long life. But I told him that in forty years time we'll all be living on the moon and living to three hundred. I'll be dying at the prime of my life.

"But wait a minute," he pointed out. "Let's not forget that she also said that you would be married next year. So if you're not married next year, that proves she's a fraud, and then you won't die at eighty-eight."

His logic was perfect. Which means I've got fifteen more months to party. And then I can go back on JDate.

Job Loyalty

It was only after I left the world of investment banking, that my resume's long list of employers became an issue. During an interview for a position at a media conglomerate, my inquisitor probed into what he perceived as a flaw in my character. "Where's your loyalty?" he asked. I was surprised by the question and explained that job switching was typical of my former industry. But if I were in a similar situation today, I would simply say, "Have you heard of the 2008 financial crisis?" Where was management's loyalty to its employees when it took the risks that cost them their jobs?

There are two simple pieces of advice I always give to young workers. Loyalty works two ways and you must always leave your first job. That's because your very first boss will never value you the way strangers do. He'll always see you as that fresh-out of-school putz asking all those stupid questions.

My very first real job was as a research assistant at a boutique stockbroker in Toronto. I slaved eighty-hour weeks for a senior analyst who did not know how to build a spreadsheet and who cut his toenails at his desk. I neglected my social life and my studies — I was trying to do the CFA program in my off hours, something he felt was a waste of time. After two years on the job, I walked into the office to discover that he had created a junior analyst position just above me — which he had already filled. I asked him why had he not considered me for the role? He said, "You don't have the experience." I quit the next day, moved to Hong Kong, and within five years was earning more than him.

I learned from that lesson and changed companies three times in my first nine years in Hong Kong. My moves were strategic as well as financial. To this day I am proud of the fact that I always remained on good terms with my previous employers. That's because I treated them with respect in never accepting a new job without giving them the chance to counter.

But there was another reason I left, I must admit. An analyst's career is exceptionally demanding; I typically arrived in the office before 6:45 a.m. and was lucky to get out by 7:00 p.m. I worked most weekends and took few holidays. This was the real reason why I changed companies so often. Every time I switched firms, I negotiated two months off before the start date, which I spent dozing on a beach.

Another lesson in misplaced loyalty came from my company expense account. My first boss had given me a speech about cost control, and it stuck. In my early years as an analyst, I treated company expenses like my own — frugal to a fault. During business trips, I never even opened the hotel mini-bar, instead buying my soda at the 7-11. I ate breakfast at Starbucks and tediously entered the digits from a calling card into the hotel phone for international calls.

And then I learned I was doing it wrong. I was in

Switzerland on business and one of the sales guys invited me to join him at the hotel's French restaurant for dinner. I told him I wasn't hungry — I'd already had my Big Mac. Still, he suggested I at least join him for a drink. So, I sat down with him just as he was finishing his escargots with garlic butter. I gave him a rundown on my presentation as he cut into roasted pheasant with seared foie gras. I fielded his uninformed questions as he swallowed chocolate ginger truffle tart with caramelized mango and sipped a double espresso. But the coup d'état was his after-dinner drink. I could barely utter a word after I saw him order a hundred dollar glass of 1968 Bowmore Islay Single Malt. And here I was, washing my underwear in the hotel sink.

By 1998, I was successful, cynical and nearing the two-year mark at my company. I was still in Hong Kong and was approached by a US boutique bank, which was expanding its activities into Asia. My interviewer and soon-to-be boss offered me an exceptional package — significantly more than I was earning at the time. The catch? Excellent compensation aside, resources would be limited. So whereas I had a team of eight analysts in my previous firm, here I would have budget for only two hires.

I guess what he was saying is that if I'm a smart guy and I'm an aggressive guy — all the things I am supposed to be if I work in this industry — then I would take this job. That's what he wanted me to think. What I was really thinking was I could never pull it off. But the money was too good to be true.

I asked him how long his bosses were budgeting for Asia to turn a profit? "Oh, about two years," he said.

"That's perfect," I thought but did not say. The business model had little chance in my mind. But I reckoned I had only about two years left in me anyways before I completely burned out. This was the first time I have taken a job for the wrong reason, assuming it's wrong to sell out. So I hired a lawyer to ensure I was protected if everything went belly up. I then took my requisite two-month holiday.

My new employer was new to Asia and did not yet have many clients. So, I had a lot more free time than I had anticipated. In fact, all I really remember about my first month on the job is renovating my apartment. I remember a lot of long lunches in my second month. My friends could not believe my new life. I was a new man: happy, refreshed and fit. You see, I was also going to the gym daily. And the job itself? Healthy body breeds healthy mind, and I was surprised to see myself enjoying my work once again. Maybe I would not have to quit for a holiday after all.

We were making strong inroads into the market but

unfortunately the good times ended soon after. Less than two years after I joined, my prediction came true. I walked into the office to discover it was all over. We had been acquired. Given that the acquirer had a research department of its own, most of us moved on. Fortunately, the job market was hot and we were compensated for the inconvenience.

Loyalty is a tricky subject when it comes to work. What's best for the company, and what's best for the boss, may prove downright awful for its employees. And those employees who stay loyal to a fault? Hopefully, their loyalty is placed in equally loyal hands. Otherwise, they might consider a career in dry-cleaning, where they can put their underwear washing skills to good use.

Niagara Falls Is No Big Deal

I am worried for our children. I am worried for our society. I am worried for our future. I think we have an impending crisis on our hands.

I am troubled by pornography and the impact it may have on our youth. It's not that I'm a prude. I've certainly seen my fair share of porn over the years. But it was not easily obtained. The anonymity of the internet has changed everything. Any child with a computer and an internet connection can instantly access the most explicit and hard-core sexual images imaginable.

And why is that a bad thing?

Jeff Goldblum, in a speech at the end of the movie *Jurassic Park*, said it best — although he was talking about dinosaurs, and I am talking about naked women. His words:

'The problem with scientific power you've used is it didn't require

any discipline to attain it. You read what others had done and you took the next step. You didn't earn the knowledge yourselves, so you don't take the responsibility for it. You stood on the shoulders of geniuses to accomplish something as fast as you could."

He was right. Unlike today's young lads, my generation had to earn its knowledge. This was easier said than done. When I was a kid, if I wanted to see a naked woman, I did what other boys did; I walked into a 7-11 and bought a *Playboy*.

This was no easy task, particularly if you were as shy as I was. So, I'd wait till the wee hours of the morning — one o'clock was ideal on a weekday night — to sneak off to the store. I wanted no witnesses to my wickedness. If there happened to be another civilian inside, I'd walk up and down the aisles eying cat food, cereal and candy bars as I avoided the inevitable. I'd flip through *The Economist* or *Time Magazine*, all while watching the clerk out of the corner of my eye, and waiting for that opportunity when there was nobody else at the counter. I would then grab a *Playboy*, rush the counter, hand the clerk exact change and head out into the night.

This wasn't much fun and it was for that that reason I was a big fan of Montreal's long and cold winters. Not because I was into skiing. Rather, because I could wear my ski mask into the store, and nobody would look twice.

What's more, unlike the kids of today, I did not get to see pornographic videos when I was young. For one thing, my dad did not buy a VHS video player until I was fifteen years old. For another, I never got the courage to walk into the adult-only section of the video store. So I pitifully rented movies like Monty Python's *The Meaning of Life*, which was famous — at least among my friends — for the slow-motion (and topless) chase scene.

It was thus a slow and lengthy apprenticeship by which I gained insight into the mysteries of women. And mystery it was. Given my lack of video tutelage, hippie hairdos and the inadequate diagrams in *The Encyclopedia Britannica*, is it any wonder that it took me some ten years to figure out if the clitoris was on the top or the bottom?

But I don't see my trials and tribulations as a bad thing, quite the opposite. Pornography is kind of like coffee; the more you consume, the stronger it needs to be, in order to have an impact.

But what of our children? Considering the sort of material they can access over the internet, the kids of today will be immune to its effects before they've even finished grade nine. And if they are looking at hardcore orgies now, what will they look at when they are twenty years old? What sort of sick deviants will they be when they are my age?

And what sort of expectations will they have in their personal relationships?

Do you remember the first time you saw Niagara Falls? I only saw the real thing a few years back. And what did I think? Well, after seeing taller waterfalls in *Jurassic Park*, wider waterfalls in *Indiana Jones and the Kingdom of the Crystal Skull* and floating waterfalls in *Avatar*, all I can say is Niagara Falls was no big deal.

Time-Travel

OK, so you're on holiday somewhere exotic, let's say Cambodia. What have you got planned?

Day One

You arrive. You're exhausted. You check into your hotel. You eat dinner in the lobby restaurant and then settle into your room for the night. You flip on the TV and scan the stations, looking for something naughty. You settle on CNN and fall asleep.

Day Two

You sit down for a buffet breakfast, eat way too many cinnamon buns and then get on the bus that takes you to the Bayon Temple. You walk around, admire the dozens of Buddha-face towers and take lots of photos. You sit down for lunch with the rest of your tour group and chat with Michael and Mary from Wisconsin. After lunch, you visit the War Museum, before boarding a romantic sunset river cruise. Look who's sitting next to you: it's Michael and Mary! After dinner on the nearby strip, you grab a drink at the hotel bar before falling into a deep, dreamless sleep. An event-filled day indeed!

Day Three

You mix things up with a visit to the Ta Prohm ruins. Wow! Angelina Jolie filmed *Tomb Raider* here. You take more pictures, always careful that there are no tourists to be seen in any of your photos.

Day Four

It's the temples of Angkor Wat and then the stalactites and stalagmites of some ancient bat cave. What was the name of the cave again? You don't remember.

Day Five

You're 'templed' out so it's the hotel swimming pool and a cheeseburger. Hey, these are really good french fries, aren't they?

Day Six

You're feeling guilty for yesterday's laze at the swimming pool so you get up extra early and cram in three ancient tea ware museums before breakfast. You then do two temples in quick succession. Afternoon comes. It's so hot! Will you go to another temple? No — but you will ask the concierge if there's a movie theatre in the village. There isn't. Ok then — back to the pool.

Day Seven

You return home. You're ready to go. You can't bear to see another temple. You have loads of photos to show your friends. What a great trip!

What is it with tourists, temples and museums? In the city where I grew up, I've never even been to the museum. In fact, when I pulled out a tourist guide of my home city, I realized that I had not even done half of the things that tourists were recommended to do. So what is it about tourists that when they go to a foreign land, they spend their entire time doing things that none of the locals do? Like visiting temples, museums and waterfalls. They also spend a lot of time watching sunsets. Then they come home and tell everybody what a great time they had and their impressions of the country:

> *"You have to go to Cambodia. What can I say, the temples: awe-inspiring, spectacular, mind-boggling. The people: spiritual, friendly, down-to-earth. It really opened my eyes. This was definitely the trip of a lifetime! If you can, then you really must do it! You have to travel there before it all changes!"*

The reality is that they didn't even really travel to Cambodia. They didn't even want to travel to Cambodia. They thought they did, but they didn't. What they really wanted to do was time-travel. They wanted to see a country in its original form, back before modern civilization infringed. That's why they spent their entire vacation visiting museums and temples. You certainly did not see them visiting shoe manufacturers or textile factories.

No, people have no interest in visiting modern day Cambodia; they want to see the ancient city and they want to do it in style, with their CNN and buffet breakfast. And what's more, they want to feel like they are the only ones doing it. Like they are the first! That's why they always shoo other people out of the way when they take photographs. So their friends back home will think that they were the only ones standing in front of that temple. Like they discovered it! Everybody wants to be Marco Polo!

> *"This photo? That's the, ummm, honey, what was this temple called? The what? The Bounty Sweet ruins? Whatever ... anyways it was well off the beaten track. We had to drive off-road for four hours. We then hiked another two hours to get there. We were lucky to even see it in the first place. Tourists never go there and even most locals don't know about its existence. We had a fantastic guide though — Steve was his name. He took us to so many incredible places, but these ruins were the ultimate. They were totally overgrown with plants and trees. I think we were the first people there in months, if not years! Listen, if you do go to Cambodia, remind me and I'll pass you Steve's email address."*

Amazing. Oversized meat loafers, who back home will not even lift a leg on a moving escalator, happen to go to Cambodia and 'discover' the Banteay Srei ruins, the one place that no one else knows about. What a coincidence. And unless you do the same, then you haven't experienced the country.

Moreover, unlike Marco Polo, who was a big fan of trade, the worst thing that can happen from most vacationers' point of view is economic development.

> *"Oh my God. I can't believe how much this place has changed. We were here fifteen years ago. It was so beautiful then. If only you could have seen it! The people wore traditional dress and lived such simple lives, in harmony with nature. Now there are so many cars*

and the people dress just like us. It's such a shame!"

Finally, after they return, tourists will then have the audacity to stereotype an entire nation of people.

"Oh, and the people, they're so nice. They have no money, nothing really, but they are so happy — always smiling. It really makes you re-examine your priorities. To live so simply and have such a strong sense of spirituality."

But the only people most tourists come into contact with on their holiday (other than other tourists) are hotel staff, waiters and taxi drivers. Of course these people are nice; they're catering to tourists' every need. Except sometimes the taxi drivers blow it for their country. Or you get one too many aggressive beggars. Then what you hear is this:

"Yeah, we did not really like the people. Very selfish and materialistic. Lazy. Aggressive."

You want to visit a modern city and not time travel? I'm not sure you can do it in seven days. I'm not even sure you can do it in seven months. I'm not sure you should even want to do it, after all, it is your holiday — maybe you should relax. But if you are interested, then you've got to start doing what the locals do — and there must be a few locals who enjoy cinnamon buns and CNN.

Jesus Was A Naughty Boy

I'm not a particularly good Jew: I don't keep kosher, go to temple or observe the high holidays. I'm Jewish the way an Italian is Italian. It's more of a culture than a religion as far as I'm concerned. And while I've chosen not to practice it to any extent, I can tell you one thing. If I did practice it, it would be at the holiest of holy levels. I would be an ultra-orthodox Jew, walking around with a black hat, long sideburns and a scraggly beard. I would follow each and every one of the hundreds of explicit rules described in the Old Testament.

Now why is that? Imagine you really believed in the God of the Bible, an all-powerful being who can punish you for all eternity. If you really believed he had asked certain things of you, then would you, a puny, insignificant human being, ever consider for a moment not doing it? I certainly would do everything he asked, no matter how strange or paranoid or neurotic it seemed, because frankly, he is God and I am not. My inconvenience today is worth nothing compared to my eternal damnation somewhere down the line.

Of course, I might have to spend this life behind bars, because some of God's rules don't sit too well within our contemporary legal system:

- ➪ *"Women are unclean and unholy during their menstrual cycle. Any sex during this period is punishable by death." (Leviticus 20:18)*

- ➪ *"A son who does not obey his parents must be stoned to death." (Deuteronomy 21:18-21)*

- ➪ *"A virgin who is raped must marry her attacker while her father receives compensation." (Deuteronomy 22:28)*

- ➪ *"Women cannot teach, have a position of authority over men, and must keep quiet." (1 Timothy 2:11)*

Fortunately, I don't believe in this God of the Bible, so I don't have to do any of this crap. But I've always wondered how Jews who do believe in him justify not following his rules. Do they think Hell is just a warmer version of Miami?

While non-practicing Jews like me are potentially in for a nasty shock after we die, I can't help but fear that the same dire fate holds true for most Christian denominations who may not even know they are going to Hell. After all, nobody's been warning them that they also need to heed God's Old Testament instructions.

What I find astonishing is that few Christians respond to my dire prediction with: "We do not believe in the Old Testament!" This would satisfy me and shut me up, since I don't believe in it either.

Instead, they simply say the rules of the Old Testament do not apply to them because it was directed at the Jews.

Perhaps nobody ever told them that Jesus was a Jew,

regularly quoted from it and specifically ordered his followers to uphold it. Perhaps they were sick the day this verse was discussed back in Sunday school:

> *"Do not think that I have come to abolish the Law or the Prophets; I have not come to abolish them but to fulfill them … Anyone who breaks one of the least of these commandments and teaches others to do the same will be called least in the kingdom of heaven …" (Matthew 5: 17-19)*

If I were a God-fearing Christian, I would find it very difficult to disobey the 'least of these commandments.'

But I could never be a God-fearing Christian. That is because if I were truly God-fearing, I would have no choice but to convert to Judaism. Not because Jesus ordered his followers to uphold the laws of the Old Testament. And not because God calls the Jews his 'Chosen People' — although it is rather nice. Rather because in Revelation 7 and 14, it's revealed that the only survivors of the Apocalypse will be Jews, and only 144,000 at that:

> *"Do not harm the land or the sea or the trees until we put a seal on the foreheads of the servants of our God … the number of those who were sealed: 144,000 from all the tribes of Israel." (Revelation 7:3-4)*

I'm told there are many Christians who are not believers in Revelation. Frankly, I don't blame them. None of them survive it.

However, many Christians are believers in the Old Testament. So how do they justify not obeying God's very specific instructions? Why aren't they more concerned about the ramifications of such cavalier insubordination?

The reason is simple: Jesus said, 'No Problem!'

Except there were other times when Jesus said it would be a problem. The fact of the matter is, Jesus was a bit of a flake and was remarkably inconsistent in his teachings. It's true that on some occasions he ordered his followers to uphold the laws of the Old Testament. But on other occasions, he contended that God was establishing a new covenant with man. Many Christian denominations have taken this to mean that they can ignore the Old Testament.

This seems a rather strange conclusion for a society that has popularized television shows like *Law and Order* and *Judge Judy*. God's explicit laws were given to Moses centuries before Jesus came along. Even the occasional unseasoned television viewer would know that Moses' comments had jurisprudence.

Understand that I am not dismissing the possibility that Jesus really was the Son of God and that the New Testament is accurate. Let's assume this is 100 percent true — an unassailable fact. But where does being the Son of God give Jesus permission to override his father's commandments? Let's not forget what happened to Adam when he disobeyed God's instructions. (Although considering Deuteronomy 21:18-21 [see page 75], Adam actually got off rather lightly.) I wonder if Jesus contemplated any of this as he sunned himself on the cross?

But God gave Jesus a mandate to speak on his behalf, did he not? There is one very enlightening section in the New Testament where Jesus is on top of a mountain praying and God speaks from a cloud, commanding all present to obey Jesus! Peter, James and John all bore witness to this:

> *"About eight days after Jesus said this, he took Peter, John and James with him and went up onto a mountain to pray. As he was praying, the appearance of his face changed, and his clothes became as bright as a flash of lightning … Peter and his companions were very sleepy, but when they became fully awake, they saw his glory … While he was speaking, a cloud appeared and enveloped them … A voice came from the cloud, saying, 'This is my Son, whom I have chosen; listen to him'… The disciples kept this to themselves, and told no one at that time what they had seen." (Luke 9:28-36)*

This is also described in Matthew 17:5 and Mark 9:7. While

this might be considered hearsay in a court of law, it still seems pretty compelling evidence of Jesus' mandate from God, a mandate that effectively gave him permission to override God's Old Testament rules. And three people witnessed these events: Peter, John and his brother James.

Except a couple of things don't quite add up. Perry Mason would have had a field day cross-examining these clowns.

Before we evaluate their credibility, let's put the whole episode into context. Four guys come down from the top of a mountain with a half-baked tale of long-dead prophets and the voice of God. I say 'half-baked' because Peter and his companions were described as 'sleepy' and because they were 'enveloped' by a talking cloud. The scriptures obviously omitted the part about the cloud being exhaled from their lungs. The real question is not what they thought they saw but whether they had enough potato chips and ice cream.

Moving onto the witnesses, let us first consider Peter. Peter was one of Jesus' closest disciples and one of the few men in the history of the world to claim to have heard the voice of God.

I don't know about you, but if I was best friends with the Son of God and had personally met God, there is not a thing on this planet that could scare me! I would be like, "You can break my legs and crucify me, I don't care, because my best friend is Jesus Christ and I am going to Heaven, WOO-HOO!"

So what happens? After Jesus is arrested and taken off to be crucified, Peter disowns him to save his own skin: 'Jesus, who's Jesus? Never heard of the guy.'

> *"Then seizing him, they led him away … Peter followed at a distance. But when they had kindled a fire in the middle of the courtyard and had sat down together, Peter sat down with them. A servant girl saw him seated there in the firelight. She looked closely at him and said, 'This man was with him.' But he denied it. 'Woman, I don't know him,' he said" (Luke 22:54-58)*

Peter ultimately disavowed knowing Jesus three times! As far as I am concerned, Peter has lost the right to speak and should keep his opinions to himself.

The next witness on that mountaintop was John, the man who — most Christians believe — wrote *Revelation*. If you accept John's testimony as to what happened on top of the mountain, then you must also accept his honesty in regards to the book of

Revelation. And in case you've forgotten, that book says you're not making it into heaven unless you're one of 144,000 Jews. Sorry.

Still, the key question is not whether Christians are making it into Heaven. Rather, the question is, did Jesus actually get a mandate from God on that mountaintop? How credible is John as a witness?

John was the youngest of the disciples and loyal to a fault. Did he have reason to lie? As anyone who saw the movie *Brokeback Mountain* knows, being alone on top of a mountain can leave even the hardiest of men feeling a little bit lonely, and perhaps a little more open-minded. In his own gospel, John likes to remind the readers that he was the 'disciple that Jesus loved.' He mentions it four times to be precise. That's a lot of loving!

Brokeback Mountain tells the story of two men who found love on top of a mountain. On Jesus' mountaintop, there were four men. Now that would be a movie worth seeing. Perhaps Mel Gibson could direct this one and call it, *The Passion of the Christ – The Prequel.* The movie could begin with Morgan Freeman or James Earl Jones reading from that curious last passage in Luke, just after the cloud had enveloped the four men:

> *"The disciples kept this to themselves, and told no one at the time what they had seen." (Luke 9:36)*

The last witness is James, John's older brother. I must admit that I cannot find any dirt on him. But he could hardly be described as objective. James knew Jesus longer than just about any other disciple and was often seen loafing around with John and Peter, who've I've already discredited. In other words, all the witnesses come from the same gang.

So, Jesus may well have been the Son of God, but there is clearly insufficient evidence to prove that he had a mandate to discard God's rules. Many Christians will disagree with me. Moreover, they might argue that Jesus is in fact the embodiment of God rather than simply being his son. By their logic, the word of Jesus is no different than the word of God. God was simply presenting a new covenant. That is within his right; after all, God is God.

I cannot find a flaw with this logic if this is indeed what you believe.

However, this raises a new question. Why would someone who knows absolutely everything about everything suddenly change his mind about how we should govern our lives? One second we've got Moses telling us don't eat pork and the next second we've got Jesus telling us all we need is love. We're only talking about 1200 years from the time Moses lived to the time Jesus lived, a drop in the bucket for a God who lives for all eternity. Here's what Moses had to say on this matter back when God's Old Testament laws were first given:

> *"However, if you do not obey the LORD your God and do not carefully follow all his commands and decrees I am giving you today, all these curses will come upon you and overtake you. You will be cursed in the city and cursed in the country … The LORD will send on you curses, confusion and rebuke in everything you put your hand to, until you are destroyed …" (Deuteronomy 28:15-20)*

Cursed in the city and cursed in the country? Seems pretty clear to me. It doesn't appear that God is going to be changing his mind any time soon with a new covenant. Moreover, if God has in fact changed his mind, it does not take a psychology degree to realize he has 'issues' and is probably not the best authority figure.

So it would appear, that at the end of the day, Christians and secular Jews (like me) are going straight to Hell for our blasphemous biblical revisions. Still, I find that less frightening than the alternative. Because if you're wondering why I haven't criticized Islam it's quite simply because the problem there is just the opposite: there's not enough revision. And that's all I'm saying on this subject because I can do without a Jihad on my head, thank you very much.

I'm Special

Next time you're in a restaurant take a good look around the room. How many of those assholes look special to you? Is the fat slob digging into that cheesecake special? What about the old guy in the expensive suit with the girlfriend twenty years his junior? Are they special? And what about the waiter who forgot your french fries? Is he special too?

I ask this question because no doubt most of these schmoes grew up with their mom and dad telling them that they are in fact special, a champion, destined for greatness. But how can everyone be special?

When I see parents relentlessly spotlighting their kids, trumpeting their every action, I have to wonder if perhaps we've lost our way. I challenge the wisdom of championing every karate punch thrown or picture drawn, especially since most children couldn't defend themselves against a turkey, and let's face it, gluing macaroni to a piece of bristle board is not exactly Michelangelo.

I am not saying that you should not instill confidence and support your children in their development. But what concerns me is the indulgence and entitlement that often goes hand in hand with parenting today. Today's privileged children walk around like little emperors, wearing designer clothing and trying out expensive new hobbies as if they were jeans — designer jeans that is.

Now, before the ubiquitous child-rearing expert tries to tell us that today's kids are no more spoiled than previous generations, consider this evidence, sourced from several thick books which I skimmed and have not footnoted:

- *Two thirds of children between the ages of eight and eighteen have televisions in their bedrooms.*

- *A global survey of seventy cities found that 61 percent of American tweens — more than any other country — want to be famous.*

- *By 2004, total advertising and marketing spending aimed at children is estimated to have reached 15 billion dollars, up from only 100 million dollars twenty years earlier.*

- *Children twelve and under influenced family purchases to the extent of approximately 200 billion dollars in 2000 up from 5 billion dollars in 1960.*

- *Demographics and inflation are not enough to explain these dramatic increases.*

Now, assuming we can agree that kids today are indeed more spoiled than our grandparents' generation why is that necessarily a bad thing? I have to admit that kids look pretty damn happy playing their video games and running around like a bunch of maniacs. There is certainly no scientific basis that I have found (or more accurately, bothered to look for) which would suggest that telling your kids they are special could be harmful. But something does not feel right. After all, divorce rates at 55 percent in North America are at an unprecedented high.

Might there be a correlation? Well, what happens when spoiled children grow up? From the moment you are born, your family tells you that you are special, that you are a treasure, that you can do no wrong. Do you think that that when you spend your entire childhood feeling special that this could perhaps have an impact on your ability to socialize effectively when you get older?

And there is an even greater issue.

Consider me as a case in point. When I was a boy, I was arguably spoiled. And self-absorbed too! For instance, I could not tell you my parents' date of birth if my life depended on it, but I always demanded special treatment and attention on my own birthday. I would skip down the hallway before my party began, singing my own personalized rendition of Lesley Gore's 1963 hit song, *It's My Party*. My rendition went something like this:

> *"It's my party and you'll cry if I want you to,*
> *Cry when I trick you,*
> *Cry when I kick you …"*

Or something like that. Then, once my birthday party started, I would zig and zag, bossing other kids around, snorting snacks, basking in my glory. When an adult gave me a present, I would snatch it away greedily. But did I ever reciprocate on their birthday? Did I ever give them a proper thank-you, before I staggered off with my loot with that greenish glint in my eye? No, because I was the special one.

So, when it comes to my nephews, I don't want them to follow in my footsteps. That's why I make no attempt to remember their birthdays. When their birthday rolls around, and they ask me where their gift is, I smile and say, "You'll get your gift when I get my gift. Do you even know when my birthday is?"

They never do. So they get nothing. I don't want them to have any false illusions. After all, isn't it about time they realized that I'm the one who's special?

The Best Thing That Ever Happened To Me

There is a small part of me that believes that parents are playing a collective practical joke on all us childless folk:

> *'Oh yes, we used to be just like you. We used to hate other people's kids too, but once you have your own, you'll see it's different.''*

It's the perfect argument, because I cannot understand how great kids are until I make the commitment. But by then it'll be too late. What if it's not different? What if I end up having a kid, and my child-bearing friends come up to me with tears in their eyes and put their arms around me laughing, "Gotcha!"

When it comes to having kids, women get more harassment than men. But as a single, forty-year-old man, I've gotten my share of pestering. I've never actually given the matter a lot of thought. Children are a huge responsibility and a decision of this magnitude should not be made by a person who's yet to figure out how to iron a shirt. Besides, I can't do it on my own.

Fortunately, I have some time to find me a wife just yet. Only recently divorced, I don't have to make a quick decision. Since my wife was the one that ended it, I am supposedly suffering and in great pain. This means I can do whatever I want and society — in other words, my friend's wives — will tolerate me. I reckon I've got at least two years to play around before these same wives decide that I need to get my shit together.

I've got to be careful though that I don't wait too long. Because, when it comes to having kids, society can forgive me for being divorced, but it can never forgive me if I choose not to have kids. I'll be branded for the rest of eternity as self-absorbed, selfish, and somebody to be avoided.

I could probably handle society's scorn if it kept quiet about it. But when it comes to having children, everybody feels they have the right to chime in:

- ➪ *"Until you have children you can't understand. I was like you. I did not want kids either. But trust me, it's the best thing that ever happened to me."*

- ➪ *"To be perfectly frank, I think it's incredibly selfish of you. It's important to give something back to society."*

- ➪ *"That's what we were put on this earth for. In the end, it's what we were made for."*

Now why is that? Why should society care about us childless folk? After all, it's not just friends who give us grief, but complete strangers. Why can't these people just mind their own business?

The answer is simple. Parents are happy. They're so happy they could just burst. And if they're happy then God darn it, we should be so happy too.

How nice that they should care about my happiness. That is too kind. The funny thing is, I don't remember any of them coming to support me when I tried standup for the first time at Yuk Yuks. Nor do I recall a phone call to see how I was doing after I broke that leg. And I certainly don't remember them wishing my cat 'Happy Birthday,' or being thrilled for me when I had that one-night stand with their sister. The truth is, I don't remember them giving a crap about me any other day of the week. But suddenly they care enough about me to ensure I have a kid one day. Just like them.

While every parent you meet will tell you that their children are the best things that ever happened to them, something feels wrong. Can you think of anything else in the world that every single person on the planet would endorse? I like hamburgers and so do most people but not everybody. Marriage is liked by many but not everybody, witness the divorce rates. Sunny days?

You would think that everyone loves them, but ask farmers, vampires and albinos. Chocolate? Beaches? Movies? Dogs? Cats? And what about parents — does everyone love their parents? I don't think so. So why should I believe that every parent loves their children?

Besides, if having children is so great, then why do all my friends who have kids always seem so bummed about my social life?

One spectacular New Year's Eve comes to mind. The following day, Howard called me up a little too early and glibly inquired as to my health — was I still alive? Howard had not been invited to the party and imagined it to be a drug-filled orgiastic frenzy. I ignored his question and asked him what he got up to?

"We had dinner with some parents from Susie's playgroup."

I could certainly understand why he was a little miffed. The fact that he described them as 'parents' rather than 'friends' suggested they were perhaps not the most interesting folk. Still, I was surprised by his resentment. After all, I spent the night with a complete stranger. He had the 'best thing that ever happened to him' to keep him occupied when he got home.

But the reality is there is another reason that the world's parents require the rest of us to have children. It's a sign of our humanity, our morality. To do otherwise is selfish.

This would make sense if it were not for the fact that it makes no sense. Yes, it is indeed selfless to take care of a child. I completely concur. However, it is selfish to create that child in the first place. If future parents truly wanted to be selfless, they would adopt a child instead of growing a new one. There are plenty of children suffering in the world. I don't need to show you any statistics here.

But my arguments are irrelevant because genetic propagation is what we were put on this earth for. It's the meaning of life. It's our genetic destiny. Seven billion people are simply not enough. We could all die out any day. So let's focus on breeding. That's our social responsibility. We weren't put on this earth to create music, art or literature. We weren't put here to build skyscrapers, cure diseases or develop exciting new technologies. We weren't put here to make people laugh or help those already-born human beings that are less fortunate than ourselves.

Perhaps Mother Teresa should have abandoned the children of Calcutta and had a few of her own. And what about those other non-contributors to the gene pool: Oprah Winfrey, Leonardo Da Vinci, Sir Isaac Newton, Dr. Seuss and Jesus Christ? Talk about selfish.

True Love Exposed

Yesterday I fell in love. She was working out at my gym, Diesel Fitness, which has a reputation for its attractive female members. She wasn't over the top beautiful. She was quiet and had an intelligent look to her. I figured she was a doctor or a robotics engineer. I saw another member talking to her, and afterwards I went up to him and asked him what her deal was?

"Oh, Angel? She's a stripper."

"What!" I was completely taken aback. At least she wasn't a lawyer. But I was still less than pleased. "She's a stripper? No! She seems so nice. So sweet!"

"Yeah. She is nice."

"Nice? How's she nice?"

"Whenever I go to Club Paradise, she always tells me who gives the best lap dances."

I was heartbroken. The love of my life grinding some guy in a club, when she could be worshiping me.

I always feel a little sad when I find out a woman is a stripper. (Not that this has happened all that often.) It's not because I have a problem with stripping per se. Rather, I feel bad because I wonder what sort of normal life a woman could have if she works as a stripper. Coming face-to-thong each day with men's depravity, I imagine she could never have a fulfilling relationship and would eventually grow to hate all men.

Then it occurs to me that I have no idea what a stripper would actually think, because I've never actually spoken with a stripper — outside of a strip club. For all I know, it could be liberating.

While I don't really believe this, I pretend it's true. I imagine Angel and I sharing our lives, happily married and living in Forest Hill.

During the day, I'd putter away on my laptop while she'd lie in the backyard tanning and reading a copy of *Bonsai Bush*, the Japanese periodical with all the latest stripper grooming fashions. In the evenings, I'd visit her at the club, bringing a thermos of hot chocolate or chicken soup. And family? We'd have a dog and a cat and of course twins: a boy and a girl. We would raise our children in an open and honest environment. We would have lively debates over dinner about the latest Bush member to take the presidency or the economic implications of escalating wax prices. Angel would teach our daughter, Angela, the importance of pole hygiene: "Always bring your own wet naps, sweetie." I would teach our son, Louis, the importance of entering a strip club first: "This way your friends get stuck paying the bouncer's tip."

Life goes on. Angela turns eighteen and moves to Niagara Falls — where lap dances still command a five-dollar premium. Louis lives at home until he's thirty before moving to Montreal to study at the prestigious linguistics center, the Gentlemen's

Club MC Academy. My heart is bursting with pride at our children's accomplishments. Life has been good to me.

The seasons pass and I go gray-er. My muscles shrink and between my hernia, my plantar fasciitis and my arthritic shoulder, I can no longer workout let alone bench press 215 pounds for three sets of twelve repetitions. Instead, I focus on my daily walks, once a day around the block. I smile and make eye contact with every person I pass during my ninety-minute regime. Must keep moving. Don't feel sorry for me. My eyes twinkle.

One day I come home from my morning workout to see Angel lying on her side in a puddle of clear liquid. She is unconscious. She has broken her hip doing her morning exercises and, in the fall, burst a saline pack. When she returns from the hospital, she is changed. She is not the same person she was before. She walks with a limp, shoulders stooped, head down. But her eyes are wild. Her memory is fragmented: Alzheimer's.

We spend our golden years sitting in the park holding hands and looking off into nothing. Young couples walk by. They smile at us two old lovers, before scurrying away in fear when Angel opens her legs at them, cackling wildly.

And then I get a phone call. It's the police. Angel is inside a subway car. She is upside down, hanging from one of those poles that lead from floor to ceiling and she is refusing to move. Two policemen try to forcefully remove her but they cannot. The power of her stripper thighs has not diminished despite her age. It's always the last thing to go, they say. I arrive and plead with her to come down. But she is crying and says repeatedly that she can't come down until they play Joan Jett's *I love Rock and Roll*. The police are concerned. There is no music playing. Besides, China is now the world's sole economic and cultural superpower. Everyone's listening to Cantonese opera-pop nowadays; it's the law. Angel's clearly lost her mind. They want to put her away in a nursing home. No, I beg them. Nursing homes are 80 percent women, and Angel's never liked woman-on-woman action.

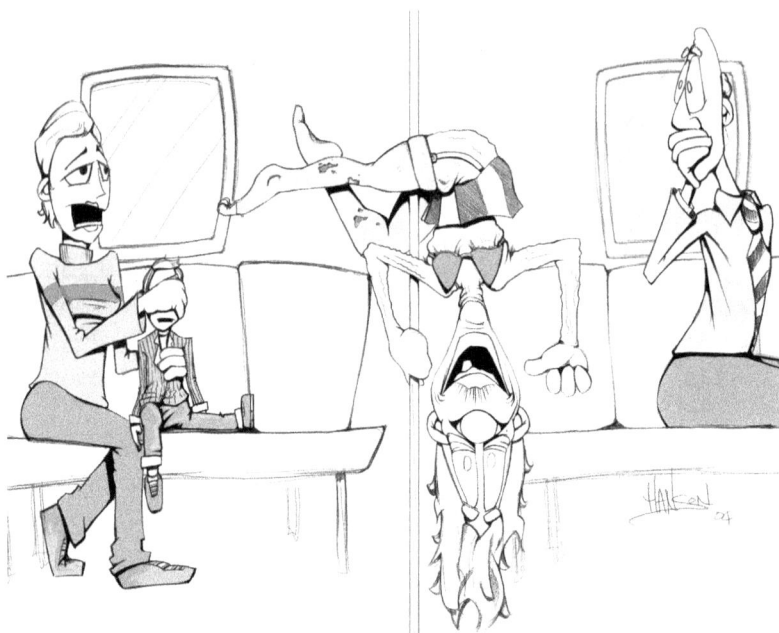

But they do not listen to me. Angel is locked away. Less than a year passes before she dies. I am left alone with my thoughts … and my memories. The days are difficult, the nights impossible. I find ways to pass the lonely evenings. I call old friends. We return to her former workplace. It has changed so much! I am amazed at the talent of these proud, young performers as they zoom above me on their bam-bam hoverstages with hydroponic stirrups. What will they come up with next? But despite all these newfangled gimmicks and accessories, I am relieved to see something that I had thought gone forever. The bush is finally back in all its 1970's *Devil in Miss Jones* glory. The Brazilians had not killed it, after all.

I smile to myself. What comes around goes around. Angel was a good woman. She was a good wife. I had a good life. Life goes on. And my friends tipped the bouncer.

Only Good People Do Yoga

About a year and a half ago, I took up yoga. I know, I know, but before any men start laughing at me, let me preface your snickers by saying that yoga is one of the hardest physical activities I have ever tried. Lifting weights is one thing; I bench press 215 pounds. But try holding your arms up for five minutes solid when you're in 'Warrior' pose; until you do that, you can shut your mouth.

I've been told that there are supposed to be many muscles in a person's back and shoulders. I say, 'supposed to be,' because in my case they had coagulated into one hard, immovable mass. A few weeks after I started yoga, I felt them loosen. It was a liberating experience. Progress has been ever so slow but I don't think I have ever done anything that felt so necessary. That was, until I did an Ana Forrest yoga workshop.

Ana Forrest is a celebrity in the yoga world and is notorious for her vigorous, intense approach to training. She suffered physical abuse and drug addiction as a young woman, and yoga helped her overcome these hardships. And here she was, coming to my studio to offer four three-hour intensive classes.

Having practiced yoga for only about a year at that time, I felt her class would be way out of my league. But as she was giving a demonstration, I stopped by the studio to watch. She was incredible, like an acrobat out of Cirque de Soleil. I was so inspired that I signed up for a three-hour slot the next morning.

Before the Saturday morning class began, Ana offered a few words of encouragement. She spoke of the spirituality of yoga and how its practice offers a release for our problems. She spoke of years of emotional issues that are literally trapped in our bodies: tension caught in our shoulders, backs, and hips. Yoga would help us deal with these problems.

I looked around the room. Many of the participants in the class were yoga instructors themselves. I knew quite a few of them on a personal level. And while they do smile a little too much, I can assure you they're no more screwed up than the rest of us. However, these were the most flexible people on the planet. If they still have emotional blockages in their bodies, then what help can yoga provide for the rest of us? I guess we all need to stretch some more.

During the class, Ana took us through complex permutations of the basic postures I was familiar with. After we struggled into a pose, she would guide us into advanced variations. I watched the director of my studio grunting as he struggled to get into one particular pose that was impossible for 99 percent of the room. I cannot remember the name of that pose. I had stalled at the first level of 'Pigeon Pose' and was unable to move even an eyebrow without tearing a hamstring. He was about five stages beyond me. I think the posture he was doing was called 'Pigeon Whimpering As Its Wings Are Pulled Off,' or something to that effect.

I was destroyed by that class. As I lay in bed that night, barely able to move, I kept thinking of these incredibly flexible people straining to become even more so. This constant need to go deeper and deeper. But to what end? Who the hell needs to be that stretchy? Is being able to do a 'Full Lotus' going to help me do anything in life other than a 'Full Lotus?'

I have often felt that yogis are a little too loose in their choice of words: 'Yoga can do this for you and yoga can do that for you.' I can't say that I have ever really bought into the so-called spiritual element of yoga. Unless you were to define 'spiritual' as the overuse of words like 'energy,' 'toxins' and 'spiritual.' Yoga would then most definitely be spiritual, because yoga instructors use those words a lot.

Religious claims aside, I do still enjoy yoga. I take out of it what I want and discard the rest. And it certainly has other advantages. Like the time I was at a bar with one of my yoga friends, David. We had been hanging out the whole day, and were still wearing our wife-beaters. We were also drinking pretty heavily. I made eye contact with a cute redhead across the room. No words were spoken, but the evening progressed and a few hours later, I stumbled into her on the street. We started talking; she asked if I was a yoga instructor. I guess it was the wife-beater. I told her no and suggested we get together for a drink some time.

"Sure! If you're friends with David, you must be a great guy," she said.

"Oh, you know David, how do you know David?"

"Oh, I don't really know him. I work in photography and have seen him a couple of times. But he seems super-cool."

Whoa. Wait a minute. Now David is a good friend of mine, and the truth is, he is a great guy. But how does she know that? What the fuck? Because he does yoga, he's automatically a great guy? You're telling me there are no assholes, no slimy guys doing yoga? He's not Gandhi; he's just stretching for fuck's sake. Unfortunately for me, I shared these views with her. So I went home alone. Yoga can do a lot for you; now if only it had taught me when to keep my big mouth shut.

Self-Reliance

On August 28, 2007, I learned that I was truly alone in this world. For it was on this day that I was cast-off by the people I thought were my friends, abandoned in the desert, while sixty miles an hour winds created a sandstorm as impenetrable as a blizzard.

This was supposed to be time of my life. I was at the annual celebration of self-expression and eco-awareness known as Burning Man. This festival numbers 48,000 participants and runs for one week in Black Rock City in Nevada.

Black Rock City is really no more than a massive campground in the middle of the desert. The 'town' does not exist before the week of Burning Man and all traces of its existence are removed at the end. Aside from security and essential infrastructure, the organizers of the event provide little. Participants must bring their own food, water, housing and entertainment.

Festival does not describe the event accurately; a more apt portrait can be painted by describing attendees' wardrobe selections. By my best guestimate, forty percent of Black Rock City's inhabitants were dressed like something out of *Mad Max*. Twenty percent were dressed like they'd walked out of *Star Wars: Episode IV*. Twenty percent were dressed for a rave. Fourteen percent were in some whacked-out Halloween costume. Just under one percent were naked. Oh and the rest were dressed like me — nerds who had no idea what the festival was about until they got there.

Burning Man gets its name from the burning of the giant wooden man at the end of the week. But I think the event should be called Sand Man, because sand was the name of the game coating every square inch of our bodies and possessions. With sand storms a regular event, balaclavas, goggles and wet naps were worth their weight in gold.

While the Eskimos reputedly have eleven different words for snow, there are dozens of names for the distinct types of sand at Burning Man. For me, three stood out:

⇨ *Schmiffins: the powdery, effervescent layer of sand that coats the inside of your tent and mushrooms into the air should you touch the fabric.*

⇨ *Schlough-schlough: the symbiotic layer of sand that coats your throat and stomach, protecting you from the grittier and coarser sand that abounds during a sand storm (see 'ohschit').*

⇨ *Ohschit: Foul, gritty sand coming right at you. Only seen in sand storms.*

My first experience with ohschit was on the second-to-last day of the festival. I was alone, on the edge of the city, when the sandstorm engulfed me. With virtually no visibility, it took me some three hours to find my way back to my campground, a journey that normally took twenty minutes.

To put my adventure in perspective, you need to understand Black Rock City. Shaped like a 'U,' it is seven square miles in size and located in an ancient dried up lakebed — the playa — one of the flattest parts of the United States. Smack in the middle of the "U" is a massive open space which leads off into the vast desert. There is no real danger though of getting lost as perimeter fences box in wayward wanderers.

My friends and I were relaxing in a tented lounge on the edge of the open space when some rangers drove by and warned us that a huge storm was about to hit. We jumped to our feet and ran to our bicycles in a bid to get back to our home camp before the storm engulfed us.

I was slow off the mark and was still trying to get my bicycle lock undone when they took off. "Hang on," I shouted. Ironically, it was the guy I knew least well that tried to wait for me. He soon turned and fled as he saw his girlfriend's pigtails disappearing in the distance. I finally got my lock off and pedaled furiously in the direction they had gone. The edge of the storm was upon us and visibility was now only twenty feet. I arrived at an intersection with no idea which way they had gone. Perhaps I should have paid greater attention to the map instead of always blindly following the group.

My sense of direction was muddled and I asked a giant ewok riding a bicycle which way to my campsite. It told me I would never make it and to find cover fast. So I turned around, meaning to return to the lounge from whence I had just departed. But it was too late. The storm was now fully upon us and visibility was only ten feet, perhaps less. The winds were so strong I had to get off my bike to push it. I never found the lounge and walked right past it into the cold emptiness of the playa.

As I walked through the swirling sands, I thought about how scary it must be to be truly lost in the desert, abandoned by the people you most trust. I self-righteously attempted to work myself into anger at my disloyal friends. But it was hard for me to get too upset. It's difficult to convince yourself that your life is in danger when every few minutes a topless Little Bo Peep or some other costumed curiosity goes running by.

My balaclava was wrapped around my nose and mouth but my eyes were still stinging badly from ohschit. I was only wearing sunglasses, having forgotten my airtight desert goggles when we headed out that morning. My eyes started to water and my vision blurred. It was at that moment that I had a vision, a flashback to a painful memory from some fifteen years earlier. I suddenly recalled another moment when my faith in my brothers was breached.

A bunch of friends and I had gotten together to play paintball, our first time ever. Before the game begun, as part of our instruction, the company rep announced we would have one practice round where we could test our skills against his. He would hide in the training zone and do combat against our entire unit. One man against fifteen. Foreshadowing aside, I think I can safely say that this was more for his masochistic pleasure than any training benefit it might provide.

I should also add at this point in the story that at least two-thirds of the fifteen members of our paintball unit were Jewish. I bring this up not because I'm a self-hating Jew, but because for the life of me I cannot understand how Israel could have developed one of the most impressive armies in the world when the ten of us were so incompetent when it came to paintball.

The game was on! We slowly inched forward, a tightly huddled mass, which I can now say with the benefit of hindsight is not the best strategy when dealing with a single armed foe. We rounded a corner and suddenly our enemy stood up from behind a single boulder, not twenty feet away from us, and dispatched one member of our group with a shot to the chest. The sniper then dropped behind the same rock as we pulled our hair and rent our clothing at the sudden cruel loss of Mordechai.

Seconds later, another overly enthusiastic member of my team peeked his nose around the corner and was taken out by a shot to the facemask. He would never daven again. There were now only eight Jews left.

We huddled to the ground, our thin necks quivering as we debated our options in the tradition of the great religious philosophers of our history. However, while the esteemed Rashi and his successor, Rashbam, made excellent points as to the appropriate interpretation of the Talmud, I don't think their non-stop gabbing would have been very useful in a game of paintball.

I suddenly had an epiphany as to why chain of command is so important in armies. Why absolute discipline is necessary and commanders need to break down men's spirits. It is to ensure that soldiers obey without hesitation any order that is given. As I listened to my friends chatter and cluck away, I knew we were doomed.

"Listen to me," I shouted. "Listen to me. I have a plan. The only chance we have to beat this bastard is to work as a team. On the count of three, a small group of us need to rush to the brush over there."

I pointed to some trees that were ten feet behind the sniper. "He'll be surrounded," I said. "Between our combined forces, he won't have a chance."

I was willing to put myself in the riskier assault force in order to give us some chance of success. I also knew that my friends would never listen to my battle plan unless I was willing to sacrifice myself too. I actually didn't care if I died. I just wanted the mission to work, to prove that my years watching television had given me the skills necessary to lead an assault team to victory. I shouted at them, waving my arms frantically for added impact, "The key thing is the rest of you guys have to cover us, when the four of us get up to run!" I pointed at my three men, "You're coming with me!" I pointed at the other men, "Cover us!"

"Now on three!"

I counted to three and jumped to my feet, heart pumping. I was instantly shot in the chest. I had not even heard a single shot of cover fire. As I walked off the field, I was acutely aware that I was the only one that had stood up. "Kill zem, kill zem all," I thought with a German accent as the rest of my people were dispatched.

Coming back to this very real desert storm, even though the events of that day would seem to indicate otherwise, I could not stay angry with my friends for abandoning me in the desert. Not even after I found out that they got drunk in a bar that afternoon while I wandered the sand dunes for what felt like forty years. You see, I counted myself lucky that I learned, with no real danger to myself, the importance of self-reliance.

Oh, and revenge. For I was on kitchen duty that evening, and finally understood the etymology behind the 'sand' in 'sandwich.'

My Fact Is My Fiction

In 2003, *CSI* won The Saturn Award for Best Network Television Series. Today, with over 70 million viewers worldwide, the crime-lab drama still has a huge following. Not all lawyers are fans; they're the ones who have to deal with jurors' sometimes unrealistic expectations as to the infallibility of forensic evidence. Perhaps jurors are unaware that The Saturn Award does not honor documentaries; it honors the top works in science fiction, fantasy and horror. Oh, and *CSI* tied for the win with *Angel*, a show about a vampire.

In the same year, *The Da Vinci Code* suggested that Jesus Christ had married and fathered a child. The book was denounced by the Catholic Church, while rebuttals (over ten books published) and an accompanying media frenzy revealed a shocking amount of people saw the novel's background material as more than just fiction.

Perhaps it was because *The Da Vinci Code*'s hero, Robert Langdon, was a Harvard professor, that readers found his arguments credible. Or perhaps it was the backslapping, congratulatory conversations he had with his friend, the Oxford-educated, Sir Leigh Teabing. Both of these men were featured in a BBC documentary, which received "rave reviews." Not as impressive an accomplishment as you would think considering that no such documentary was ever aired. How could it be? Neither of these men actually exists. The documentary, the reviews, the men themselves: it's all fiction.

Ultimately, the interest and firestorm that this book created was so intense that its author, Dan Brown, had to respond. As he wrote on his website:

> *"If you read the 'FACT' page, you will see it clearly states that the documents, rituals, organization, artwork, and architecture in the novel all exist. The "FACT" page makes no statement whatsoever about any of the ancient theories discussed by fictional characters. Interpreting those ideas is left to the reader."*

So, this is a work of fiction, and these are the 'facts' — as his characters see them. Their views differ from the Catholic Church and it is the reader's job to discern if they actually have merit. There are certainly plenty of opinions out there in the real world countering Langdon's view. Isn't it interesting that in the same way that some people take the church's teachings at face value, others take the teachings of the fictional Langdon at face value? Perhaps they think he is less fictional than the alternative?

Whether it's religious history in *The Da Vinci Code* or forensic science in *CSI*, the fact of the matter is, the entertainment industry is rife with what we perceive to be facts, but might in reality be fiction. These 'facts' can slip into our consciousness, unseen and unnoticed, ultimately shaping who we are, the way that we think and the way we view the world.

Obviously, one can't expect the entertainment industry to not take liberties in order to tell a good story. Who wants to see

24's anti-terrorist agent Jack Bauer running out of battery power on his mobile phone or cursing at how slowly his PDA downloads data. We should consider ourselves lucky that *CSI* is not accurate or even worse, filmed in real-time like *24*. Otherwise, we would be sitting on our couch for half a season waiting for the forensic team to get a simple toxicology report — just like in the real world.

No, factual inaccuracies are necessary in the world of entertainment for the sake of entertainment. We don't want to see reality. But, do we really want factual inaccuracies to impact reality?

In the world of *24*, a minute on screen equals a minute in reality. Jack Bauer doesn't have enough time to eat or go to the bathroom, let alone take the time to slowly interrogate suspects.

Torture's his only option.

Not everyone is a fan. In 2006, an article in *The New Yorker* described a visit to the show by the dean of West Point and a group of experienced military and FBI interrogators. They asked the producers to stop suggesting torture is an effective tool in combating terrorism. According to the delegation, torturing an innocent person usually yields false information. They argued that the show promoted illegal and unethical behavior and was adversely affecting the training of real soldiers. "They should do a show where torture backfires," the dean said.

It's bad enough that we can't get the truth out of fiction, but we can't even seem to get the truth out of truth. It's not just novels, television and movies where the facts are distorted but also in the one place that we're supposed to get the truth: the news. In a recent Gallup poll, 49 percent of respondents said they had "not very much" or "none at all" trust in the news media.

Personally, whether it's entertainment or the news, I never know what to believe. Not knowing fact from fiction leaves my opinions like the tides, constantly shifting. I cannot distinguish reality from imagination — truth from opinion. My views seem to be a function of whatever I most recently read or viewed. One evening, I'll watch a vitriolic news update on terrorism and within minutes, I'll transform into Schwarzenegger in *Commando*, ready to do battle. The next day, I'll read a sympathetic report with a different perspective and I become the softer, gentler Schwarzenegger in *Junior*. I may have been a gun-toting killer only moments before, but I was never given the intellectual ammunition to defend that stance. My fresh viewpoint will only hold until I am once again faced with new information of which I was previously unaware. Does this happen only to me?

Passwords

I hate choosing internet passwords. I'm too paranoid to use the same password twice so I have dozens of passwords — all slight variations of the one before.

I chose my very first internet password back in 1996. It was a bright, sunny day and almost lunchtime. I was setting up a Hotmail account. Hotmail asked me for a password. I chose 'hotdog747.' I figured I would remember 'hot' because of 'hotmail.' And I would remember 'dog' because of 'hot' and because I was hungry. I chose '747' because they were the first three digits of my phone number at the time.

Eventually, I was on a different site and the next inevitable request for a password came along. So I chose a slightly different password: 'hotdogboeing.' 'Boeing' was my brain's logical leap from '747.' I figured I was being clever, since I didn't want any one entity to potentially have access to all my accounts. But then the next website password request came along, and 'hotdogboeing' became 'hotbabeboink.' And then one day, 'hotbabeboink' became 'hotbabe69.' 'hotbabe69' eventually became 'hotsoup69' — my logic being I won't have much use for babes when I'm 69 years old, but I'll be all over the hot soup.

As my website memberships grew, so did my password variations. This was not helped by the fact that Hotmail periodically required me to change my password, so three months after I chose that first password, 'hotdog747' became 'cooldog747' — and so on, and so on.

Today, I've got no idea what 95 percent of my passwords are. Luckily, all I truly need to remember is one. Hotmail is the key to my universe — my holy grail. If I forget it, I am doomed, because I spend 17 percent of my time on the internet resetting my passwords and picking up the new ones in my Hotmail inbox. I keep a reminder of my Hotmail password in a safety deposit box. Now, if I can only remember where I put the key.

Stephen Hawking's Brief History Of Lies

When I'm on vacation, you'll usually see me reading a nice, light thriller. Something I can pick up and put down at a moment's notice. Something easy on the brain. Steven King, John Grisham or Ken Follett usually work rather nicely.

Every few years, I'll be disappointed by my ordinary tastes and vow that I'll only read books that 'better myself.' I'll sniff my way through the classics at the bookstore, thumbing my nose at the bestsellers. I'll buy thought-provoking and weighty tomes like *Guns, Germs and Steel* or *The World is Flat* or the latest by Milan Kundera. I'll meander over to the cashier, front covers facing outwards, so less sophisticated customers can admire my selections and ponder their own shortcomings.

And while I rarely regret these purchases, it's probably because I rarely ever read them. The exception to this is when I decide to better myself before a long flight. Then I regret these purchases very much indeed. Midway through that flight, I'll be slumped in the darkness, eyes staring at nothing, my copy of *War and Peace* closed and bookmarked on the fifteenth page. I'll re-read every page of the in-flight magazine and curse the airline for its copies of *Golf World* and *House and Home*. I would kill for an *Esquire* or *GQ* — anything rather then return to my book.

A long flight is hard enough without bringing an obscure and unreadable book. And of all the books I've ever regretted bringing on a flight, no book stands out more than Stephen Hawking's *A Brief History of Time*.

In case you've been living on another planet or think Kim Kardasian is a good role model for girls, Stephen Hawking was the Lucasian professor of Mathematics at the University of Cambridge between 1979 and 2009. He is considered by many as the pre-eminent quantum physicist of our time and has written on cosmology, black holes and the nature of space and time. He was rendered quadriplegic by ALS, a disease that affects voluntary muscle movement. His first book, *A Brief History of Time,* was published in 1988 and spent seventy-two weeks on the New York Time's bestseller list.

I'd heard about Hawking's book years before I decided to read it. The catalyst to finally buy it was an article that stated Hawking believed in God. In fact, according to the article, not only did Hawking believe in God, but he had proven His existence in the book! Now, I was a self-professed agnostic. But here was a scientist, with one of the biggest brains to have ever existed, who believed otherwise. I had to read his book.

Before I go any further, I should probably point out that as I prepare this chapter, I have not been able to find any article in which Hawking said he believes in God. The internet, which can provide me with everything from Santa Claus' website to proof that unicorns live on Mars, has yielded me nothing. In fact, according to today's version of Wikipedia, Hawking has said he does *not* believe in God. I don't know how I messed this up, but it appears that for all these years I was wrong. I did not have to read the book. Too bad I didn't know this back then. I could have avoided much hardship.

But back in the past, my perception that Hawking believed in God got me very excited. This was not your rabbi or your priest telling you to have faith. This was one of the greatest scientists to ever live. If he had convinced himself that there was a divine creator, I had to understand why. But there was a problem. I couldn't understand the damn book.

This first time I tried to read *A Brief History of Time* was twenty years ago, on a flight from Hong Kong to Bali. It was the only book I'd brought with me. I got no further than page twenty-two. I blamed it on the 'riveting' inflight flick, *Look Who's Talking Too*.

On the return flight, I decided to give the book a serious second attempt. I did not succeed. I did not get one page further than twenty-two. Not because of distractions (the inflight film had not changed), but because my head hurt (the inflight film had not changed). Moreover, the book did not exactly flow easily into my brain. I felt like I was reading a foreign language. Nothing made sense. I even double-checked the page numbers to make sure that no pages had gone missing. Nope — the book was perfectly intact.

In the years that followed, I have picked up the book another three or four times. I always start from the very beginning and I always read it with a pencil, a dictionary and a pad of paper — so I can take notes. During my most recent attempt — five years ago — I even read it in front of my computer, so I could google any concept that I did not understand. Yet, I never got any further than page twenty-two. The first twenty-two pages of my copy are as worn as the wheels on Hawking's wheelchair, while the rest of the book is as clean and untouched as his shoes.

Now I may not be a science guy but I'm not a stupid guy

either. I graduated from McGill University with distinction. I scored in the 98th percentile on my GMAT. The fact that I decided not to get an MBA is probably indicative of even higher cognitive abilities. So I refuse to accept that I'm the problem.

Sir Arthur Conan Doyle's Sherlock Holmes once said, "When you have eliminated the impossible, whatever remains, however improbable, must be the truth."

While it may be unorthodox to take counsel from a fictional character, the brilliant Holmes' supposition still rings true to me. If I do not understand the book and I am not stupid, then the book itself must be stupid.

But what about all the rave reviews that Hawking and his book have received? How can they all be wrong?

Back in my university days, I worked as a teaching assistant and lectured in real estate finance. One portion of the course had some very complicated math. As I prepared my lecture, months after I had taken the course myself, I realized that I'd forgotten the essential principles. So what did I do? When I got to that part of the lesson, I simply said, "The math here is pretty straightforward. I'll leave it to you to do on your own time. Let's move on to the next chapter. Any questions?"

Not a single person asked me a question.

The consensus view is that Hawking is the most brilliant physicist since Einstein. But how do we know that all this praise isn't just a case of scientists not wanting to admit that they have no idea what he is saying, because they do not want to look stupid? So they worship and flatter him, and hope that nobody asks them to explain what he's saying.

Consider the possibility that Hawking isn't really the greatest living physicist but is in fact the greatest living con man. The setup could not be better. We're told Hawking cannot speak because of a tracheotomy some years back. Using head and eye movement to control a computer program, he selects words that are converted into voice via a computerized speech synthesizer. The process is very time-consuming. Just articulating fifteen words can take up to a minute. Is it any wonder then that audiences hang on his every word? And if he doesn't answer a question properly, who would dare cross-examine him? Not if they want to get away in time for lunch.

It's like *The Wizard of Oz*. And just like the wizard, if you took away Hawking's gimmicks and electronic trickery — that futuristic wheelchair and his computer voice controls — would we be left with anything other than another skinny guy who'd have trouble getting a date?

In any event, last week I bought Hawking's latest book, *A Briefer History of Time*. It says on the inside front cover, "readers have repeatedly told Professor Hawking of their great difficulty in understanding some of the book's most important concepts." So this new book is an attempt by Hawking to make his knowledge accessible to readers who could not understand the original. Nice. The book cost me thirty bucks — maybe he is brilliant after all. I'll let you know how it goes, but I'll be taking a Grisham next time I hop on a plane.

Babies And Their Sponge-Like Brains

It's Sunday afternoon and you've accepted an invitation to your friends' home for brunch. Their two-year-old, Chucky, is playing on the floor in front of the sofa. Every time you look over at your friends you see a sparkle in their eyes as they watch the future prime minister of Canada suck on your mobile phone. You eventually have to avoid eye contact altogether because the look of sweet sugary satisfaction is just too much to take.

Not surprisingly, the main topic of conversation is the vast potential of their baby:

> *"Chucky is so smart! He was toilet trained when he was only nine months old. We've been showing him Baby Einstein cards and he can already recognize most animals and musical instruments. He's advanced well ahead of his age group — What's that? You're hungry, sweetie? — Oh, that was sign language. We've taught him sign language. When he puts his fist in front of his belly it means*

he's hungry — Good boy!"

The proud parents then go on to say how children are like sponges, sucking in knowledge at light-speed-like rates. As they explain it:

> *"Did you know that babies' brains are radically different from those of adults? Their neural pathways are not yet formed. As babies learn, their brains create new connections. But this all stops when they grow up. Their ability to absorb information decreases. This is proven! That's why we've got Chucky enrolled in French and Mandarin classes, in addition to tennis, piano and Brazilian jiu-jitsu. If you don't get them started when they're kids, they'll never learn it."*

Wait a minute. You mean if I started Mandarin lessons tomorrow, I couldn't keep up with Chucky? Not that I say that out loud. I'm hardly going to win an argument with someone who believes a child prodigy would still be shitting in the bath.

But let's put things in perspective, shall we? When was the last time you had an intelligent conversation with an articulate baby? And how young was the brightest child you ever encountered? I mean 'bright' in that they impressed you, they made you think. Twelve years old? Ten years old? Younger? OK, I'm not sure I agree, but for the purposes of this discussion let's agree on eight years old.

Since when is learning to speak a language in eight years an astronomical feat? Are you telling me that you could not learn to speak Mandarin and play tennis in eight years? Of course you could, so maybe the answer is not that kids have these futuristic sponge-like brains. Maybe the answer is that they've got nothing else to think about other than eating, sleeping, pooping, playing, and crying! While you, you've got to worry about your job, your taxes, your potbelly, putting down the toilet seat and the fact that you're so damn tired all the time. That's why you haven't been able to learn Mandarin. You're got too much on your plate.

Except we all know that's not true. Even if you had all the time in the world, your Mandarin will still sound like Jackie Chan's English and your tennis swing will have all the finesse of a wobbly toddler in new shoes.

But at least you don't poop in the bath.

The War On Terror

Here is what I don't understand. A group of terrorists hijacked some planes with nothing but a few box cutters. They then crashed those planes into the pentagon and the biggest buildings in New York. A feat like that required remarkable coordination and planning. But it was not rocket science. They did not develop a nuclear weapon. They did not unleash a deadly virus. They did not commandeer the internet or steal all of Fort Knox's gold. They didn't do anything like the sophisticated terrorists that Jack Bauer fought every season on *24*.

But they still got America. They took some box cutters and some flying lessons and they hit them hard. They succeeded in part because people assumed the status quo still applied — that hijackers were not planning to die. And that is something Americans will never fall for again. Forget about the armored cockpit doors on every flight. Nowadays, if someone were to so much as lift a spoon too high during meal service, their fellow passengers would tackle them faster than a fat kid can pounce on a free bag of pretzels.

Notwithstanding this reality, as a result of this catastrophic event, we now live in perpetual fear of another terrorist attack. Security has been tightened significantly across all of the world's airports. And nowhere has this been more strongly felt than in the airports of the United States. In the old days, protection was as slack as birth control in Utah, but things are different now.

Much like the farmer who closes the barn door after the horse has bolted, today's airport regulators continue to enforce security policies that would only avert whatever the latest terrorist threat happened to be. Because of 9/11, we lost our nail clippers and have to eat our chicken with a spoon. Thanks to the shoe bomber, we have to take our shoes off and stand around in our grubby socks. And because of the most recent terrorist attempt, we're not allowed liquids, whether they're bottles of Snapple, contact lens solution or shampoo. This is no war on terror; it's a war on convenience.

Ultimately, these restrictions, while irritating, are not impairing our way of life. Nobody's going to change his or her travel plans as a result. But what if the terrorists realize the secret to success is not blowing up a plane but rather getting regulators to orchestrate another mindless restriction because of fear of them blowing up a plane? What if this new restriction actually kept people off planes altogether? The global economy would grind to a halt.

Imagine for instance, if the Taliban were to instruct a bald suicide bomber to board an airplane with explosives hidden under his hairpiece. Think of the long-term ramifications if the FAA were to then ban toupees. Thousands of middle-aged men would have to remove their hairpieces as they go through security. No more traveling for the follicularly-challenged.

Alternatively, they could take those liquid explosives that are supposedly in our water bottles and inject them into a female terrorist's lips or — for an even bigger bang — her breast implants. Security personnel would now insist on patting down every well-endowed woman in America. The consequences would be dramatic, as many women would now refuse to fly. On the brighter side, airport security personnel would become a lot more alert.

Or if they really wanted to annihilate America, the Taliban could hide explosives in a fat suit like the one Gwyneth Paltrow wore in *Shallow Hal*. Security personnel would now have to frisk every obese individual in America. All but the loneliest of fat people would refuse to fly, putting airport Cinnabons out of business.

Well two can play at that game. While it is our vanity that could ultimately prove to be our downfall, it is lack of vanity that could prove to be the terrorists' downfall.

Consider World War II. Consider the enormous cultural differences at the time between Germans, Japanese and Americans. Half a century later, could you ever imagine a war between the youth of America, Japan, and Germany? No. Impossible.

Why is that? Call it globalization or call it MTV or call it YouTube but the end result is still the same. Kids in developed countries are the same wherever you go. They look the same, dress the same, talk the same, twerk the same, watch the same movies and listen to the same rap. They even all use that same brainless, surfer-dude hand gesture, the 'shaka' sign. You know the one, where you extend your thumb and pinky, while you keep your other three fingers curled. These kids are not going to be strapping bombs to their torsos anytime soon.

So how to hurt the terrorists? Easy. Go after their kids and kill them. Kill them with kindness. In other words, let's help terrorists' children enjoy the same lifestyle our kids enjoy. And for that they'll need some spending money.

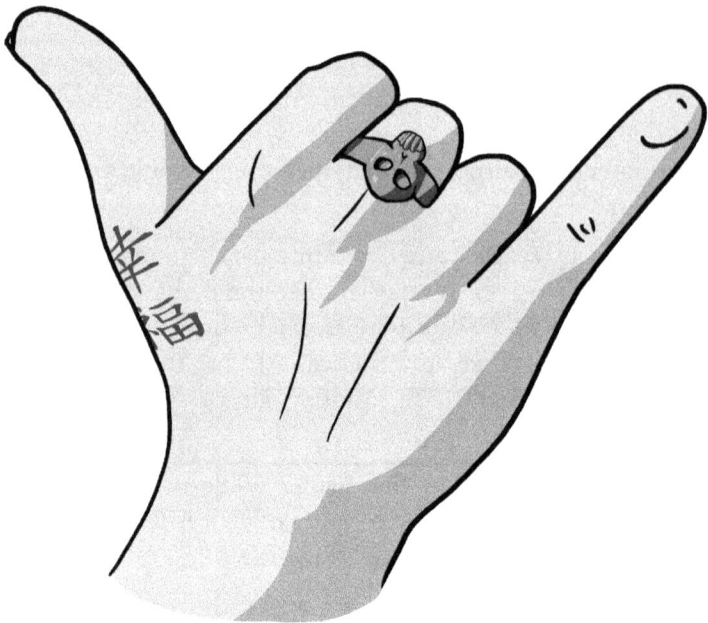

Unemployment rates throughout the Middle East and South Asia are sky high, with the youth suffering disproportionately. But if we can get the younger generation working, we can ultimately help ourselves. Because with jobs comes money and with money comes Nike sneakers, iPhones and Honda Civics with spoilers. Which solves all our problems. Because as we all know, once you've got a Honda Civic with a spoiler, you've got a hot girlfriend, and once you've got a hot girlfriend, you don't want to kill anybody.

And how to create jobs? There has been some criticism of the effectiveness of foreign aid in the Middle East and South Asia, with concerns that it might ultimately support terrorism. So perhaps the answer lies in a different set of criteria. For instance, our governments could provide financial incentives only to 'cool' Western companies like Nike, Starbucks, Apple and Disney that set up operations in troubled hot spots and employ terrorists' kids. These incentives would of course need to be large enough to mitigate the costs of a factory being blown up or Mickey Mouse being beheaded, while leaving enough cushion to earn a tidy profit.

In addition, just like humanitarian aid is airdropped into troubled disaster zones, the West could airdrop much needed hipster glasses, pork pie hats and LED hula hoops into troubled hot spots.

Could you ever imagine twenty-year-old American boys blowing themselves up so they could meet seventy-two virgins in heaven? No, that would be more like hell — especially when they have frat parties, strip clubs and spring break to enjoy in the here and now. So let's hope for a future where MTV hosts Spring Break Dance 20XX in the sun and sand of Afghanistan. Because if we give the terrorists' kids what our kids have, then the cycle of violence might finally end. Shaka signs will brim from dune to dune. Oh, and who do you think will be supplying all the party goodies? The American companies that have invested in the region — and they'll make a fortune.

Followers Of The Good Book[1]

I am standing at the Western gateway just inside the walls of Angkor Watt. It is just before sunrise and the air is cool. It has rained most of the night and the stones are wet and slippery below my feet. I am looking out in the direction of the towers some 350 meters away, but I can't see squat. It is still too dark. My back is stiff. I am tired. How much longer to wait? Shit, another twenty-five minutes until sunrise. Nowhere to go, can't see jack shit. Nothing to do but wait.

"Mee ya nay oh!"

Suddenly, I stumble forward as a shoulder jostles me hard from behind. I stagger for balance trying to avoid falling directly

---

[1] *I originally wrote this story in 2007. You might want to substitute 'iPhone app' for 'The Good Book' and 'Lonely Planet' if you are less than sixty years of age.*

onto the Japanese couple who are squatting patiently in front of me. I turn to see an overweight, middle-aged Korean man, squeezing through the crowd with his tripod, a flushed look of excitement in his face. I nod at the German just behind me and we share a look of resentment. We were here first!

Flashes start going off like firecrackers as travelers try to capture that perfect sunrise. Their photographs will look like burnt lasagna. More tourists arrive, chattering excitedly. One American lady is squeezing to the front, holding her camera directly above her head, clicking wildly in the general direction of the towers. Feeling claustrophobic, I grab my girlfriend's hand and we squeeze our way back through the crowd, to exit these walls and regain our composure.

Back-up to 11:00 p.m. the night before.

She: "Honey, I've arranged for a wake up call for four-thirty tomorrow morning."

Me: "What the Fuck? Why?"

She: "To see the Sunrise at Angkor Watt. The *Lonely Planet* says that most people go to Angkor Watt for sunset, so it suggests going at sunrise."

Me: "Oh. The Good Book says it. No problem."

Sit down in a backpacker café anywhere in the world and a *Lonely Planet* on an occupied table is as ubiquitous as an ashtray. You would think you were witnessing the birth of an intolerant religion, a fervent new cult, the way travelers obey its holy scriptures. Followers of this Good Book can be spotted instantly as they stumble through streets of a foreign land holding it in front like a cross used to ward off vampires. With the vacant look in their eyes, it could be a scene out of *Dawn of the Dead*, except here the zombies are all carrying guidebooks.

Followers of The Good Book abide by very strict laws:

Go to this temple to watch the sun rise. Go to that one to watch the sun set.

Shall we eat in this restaurant? "No! It's not in The Good Book!"

Thirsty? "The Good Book recommends the stall across the street for its banana shakes. Unless you want mango. Then it recommends this stall."

And dinner? "Oh, listen to this, 'this charming little hideaway is situated half a kilometer from the palace. The owner, Mr. Srithavatchai, oversees all cooking himself and is always ready with a good story. The prawn curry recipe was passed down from his great-grandmother and is highly recommended.' Sounds great."

'Charming little hideaway?' Maybe it was once — until it made it into the guidebook. Now you'll be lucky to be served at all, what with the two tour buses that just pulled up. That is, assuming this is the right place, because there are two restaurants with the exact same name across the street.

The truth is, even when you put your complete faith in The Good Book, there's a small part in the back of your brain that knows there's something wrong. Like when you were a kid and you wondered why there were no dinosaurs on Noah's ark.

"Honey, the Book said this club is the hottest nightspot in town. Funny though, as I look around all I see are fat middle-aged Germans."

I guess The Good Book is printed in German too.

Come Watch Me Do My Job

I'm sitting with some friends in the thirteenth row of some second-rate theatre. We're watching *As You Like It* by William Shakespeare and awaiting the appearance of our friend Roy. He has a major role in the play as the young heartthrob, Orlando. It's the fight scene, which he has also choreographed. I watch him flip his opponent to the ground like something out of the WWF. I lean forward. Now we're talking. The fighting reminds me of that scene in *Star Trek* where Captain Kirk is forced to battle Spock in the alien coliseum. All that is missing is that excellent battle music:

♫ *Da da, dah dah dah dah, da da, dah dah drrrreee! drrrreee!* ♫

Sigh … the fight scene's over. That was quick. I am so bored. I can't understand half of what is being said and I have no idea what is happening. Nor do I want to know. Granted, the actors are doing as good a job as they can possibly do, what with the dated material — all these couples in love and all of them wearing disguises. How come nobody recognizes anybody? Their disguises are worse than Clark Kent's glasses. Why am I here in the first place? Twenty-five dollars down the drain. I would never have come to this play if my friend were not in it.

What is it about friends and their plays? Why do we have to go see them? I'm told it's because 'that's what friends do, friends support friends.' So, they want me to support them in their hobbies? Well, how come they never support me in mine? I don't remember anyone clapping after I chiseled a perfect dovetail and not one standing ovation for a difficult sniper shot in *Call of Duty*.

And if acting is not just a hobby but what they actually choose to do for a living, then they're in for an even bigger treat. Because I could sure use some encouragement at my crummy job. I'd recommend a big breakfast before they arrive at my workplace though, because my show starts at 6:45 a.m. sharp and doesn't end until way past sundown.

"Oh, but the theatre is entertainment," they say. Well, I say that's a matter of perspective.

And then the play finally ends. My friends and I exchange quiet smiles and we all head outside the theatre to await his grand entrance. Roy comes out, all dressed in black. He grants me one millisecond of eye contact before his eyes dart off in other directions as he takes in his admirers. The irony is that for all the acting Roy did, we are the ones that are going to deserve an Oscar for the performance that we are about to give:

"Yes! That was great!

"I got to say, you were so believable. I literally forgot it was you. You were the character!"

"Awesome, man. Great play and you really stood out!"

And if that's not bad enough, afterwards we follow him and his actor pals to some party that is filled with even more actor friends. They're all high on booze and weed and compliments. They are talking shop and pay us no attention. I sit on the edge of the sofa. To make conversation, I turn to an actress from the play and compliment her on her performance. I get a half-smile and some uncomfortable silence before she moves off in another direction.

And of course, my acting role does not end that night. The show must go on, and my performance is on an extended run, as over the next few days, other friends ask what I thought of the play. This is most painful if Roy is in earshot when I am asked. Even if he is fully engaged in conversation with a third party, you can still see his head tilt slightly and his lips curl upwards as he waits for my scripted response: "Yeah, the play was great, and Roy … fantastic. You must see it!"

Except Roy seems less than thrilled with my follow up

remark: "But if you'd like to see a more realistic performance, I'd suggest you pop over to my workshop sometime soon; I'm building a new birdhouse."

The Gravitas Of Golf

I can remember with exquisite detail the exact moment that I gave up golf. I was not playing golf. I was not at a driving range. I was not even on a golf course. I was simply standing in front of my hotel as some friends and I waited for a taxi.

We were three friends on holiday in Scotland. Between sightseeing and partying, we were playing some of the world's most majestic courses. The game of golf was born in Scotland. Not that I deserved to be playing there. I had only taken it up a year earlier and had already spent more money on golf lessons than I had on my golf clubs, twice over. I had read all the books and consistently hit those buckets of balls. Yet I still had that hollow feeling in the pit of my stomach whenever I swung that club, that the ball was about as likely to fly true as my hotel room keycard would work, the first time I inserted it into the door.

So here I was standing on the curb in front of the hotel,

quite happy to be away from the greens. And what did I do? I started swinging that imaginary golf club, just like all the other dorks you have seen over the years.

"Your swing is all wrong!"

What? Who said that? It was the bellboy.

"Your swing is all wrong! You need to keep your arms straight and twist your body more. Use your hips!"

There are no words powerful enough to describe my anger at hearing this. This incident took place ten years ago, but even now thinking about it gets my blood boiling. I am the Sun as I write these words. I am a boiling pot of water thrown in your face. That bag-handling bastard! One millisecond after he said those words, I was done. No more golf for me. I couldn't even swing an imaginary club and get it right.

What is it about golf and the formality of it all? The pretension, the gravitas, the etiquette? Everything about the game is designed to make you feel like an asshole: inadequate, uncomfortable, incompetent. And that's before you even take that first swing; just look at the setup:

- *Stand with your feet on an imaginary line pointing in the direction you want the ball to travel.*

- *The ball should be in the center of your feet. Unless it's a long drive — then the ball should be closer to your front foot. Except if it's a short drive — then it should be off the back heel.*

- *Carefully grip your club. Place your right hand on top of your left hand, the left thumb cradled in the pad of your right hand.*

- *No, your grip is still wrong. Loosen it. Hold the club gently but firmly, like you are cradling a live bird.*

- *Your forearms should form a V-shape. Make sure you can see the first two knuckles on your right hand and the face of your watch on your left wrist.*

- *Left foot slightly out to the side.*

- *Left shoulder should be slightly lower than the right.*

- *Arms straight.*

- *Arms out about fist-length from your belt buckle.*

- *Bend your knees slightly and maintain an athletic stance. You should be able to hold an imaginary beach ball between your legs.*

- *Weight evenly distributed.*

- *Back straight.*

- *Ok, now you're ready to swing …*

Not that there's only one way to do things. You see when you're a beginner, everybody has something to say, and say it they will. As you approach the tee, bystanders will appraise you like Mr. Miyagi in *The Karate Kid*. Butterflies will do cartwheels in your stomach as you prepare your swing. Bambi on that frozen pond looks more graceful than you do as you swing that club.

And as if there wasn't enough pretension in the swing itself, the rules of golf dictate you must apologize at every hole for some protocol that you have inadvertently breached. It is as if the sport was designed to make you feel like a little kid in a tuxedo at a grown-up affair.

First of all, your clothes are all wrong. You need to go to the clubhouse right now and buy a collared shirt and some appropriate pants. I know it's eighty degrees outside but you can't wear shorts. And shoes? Cleated shoes are mandatory; you can't wear sneakers or you'll ruin the grass. But the tires from the golf cart? No problem!

Second, silence is mandatory in golf. Not a word when a golfer is putting and not a breath when he is teeing off. Hockey players expect to get checked, slashed and punched in the face. Baseball players must hit balls travelling ninety miles per hour.

Football players get trampled by 350-pound men. But golfers, they look like bowlers' ugly, inbred cousins, and yet you need to be absolutely quiet.

Third, never, ever walk in front of someone's ball once it is on the green. You'll compromise the grain. But if someone walked there before the ball landed? No problem!

And despite all the details you need to remember, you still have to play quickly because the assholes behind you —as well as the assholes you are playing with — want to finish the course in less than three-and-a-half hours.

No, we don't want to upset the assholes — i.e. the serious players. You can easily recognize the serious players at a golf course. They walk quickly between shots, have drivers even longer than they are and get angry when the ball goes 200 yards instead of 220. Moreover, they are mean. They've hit a lot of balls to get to the level they are at today so why should you — the beginner — be having any fun?

But have you ever noticed that unlike you, who only picked up golf at thirty years of age, most serious players started playing when they were just kids? Yet you fawn over them, like when you were eight and one of your classmates had potato chips and you did not. And just like that classmate, these assholes walk around like they're kings of the world, even though they have an unfair advantage. After all, we all know that kids pick up sports more easily than adults; if you doubt me, just read my chapter on babies and their sponge-like brains.

No Playmates In The Bomb Shelter

I remember participating in a group exercise back in grade seven. We were told by our teacher that there was going to be a nuclear war, one that would wipe out the entire planet. Fortunately, an impenetrable bomb shelter would survive the apocalypse. But it could only accommodate eight people. Our class had to choose its inhabitants. These would be the only survivors of the cataclysm and the future of humanity.

We weren't choosing ourselves. The teacher randomly assigned each member of the class a character, providing us with background details on occupation, age and physical traits. We would have a minute each to present our character's case to the class, before the votes were cast.

There was an interesting range of characters: a mid-forties male family doctor, a late-thirties female pharmacist, a mid-twenties male carpenter — the list goes on. The most memorable characters were two young women: one, a twenty-year-old *Playboy* playmate, who happened to be sterile; the other, a twenty-seven-year-old female engineer, who happened to be fertile.

Some of the characters got into the shelter quite easily. The family doctor got the most votes while the carpenter came in second place. The last spot was hotly contested with a tie between the barren playmate and the potentially-prolific engineer. This outraged the girls as the engineer's only apparent flaw was her resemblance to our teacher, Mr. Schwartz. Fortunately for our species' survival, the playmate was ousted in a vicious tiebreaker vote. The character assigned to me — by the way — was a mid-thirties male lawyer. Needless to say, he did not make it into the shelter either.

I think this game had a large influence on my mental development because I've always respected people who have real, demonstrable skills — 'useful' knowledge like medicine, carpentry or auto repair. The irony is that even though I value this, I never actually developed any practical skills of my own, growing up. As a young adult, I was considered rebellious enough (at least in my family) for not becoming a doctor like my brothers. Going into finance seemed risky; my parents would never have bought into me entering a trade. Especially since they knew of only one other Jew to ever do so, and aside from the annual celebration of his birthday, things didn't end too well for him.

Over the years — with no nuclear disaster to contend with — my lifelong perception that 'useful' knowledge is important has been challenged. In my years in Asia, I've seen artisans of such talent that you would think they were living the high life. They weren't.

At the same time, here in Toronto, I haven't met any carpenters living in Forest Hill either. The reality is, many talented carpenters struggle to eke out a living. It's hard to compete, when raw lumber alone costs more than a finished IKEA piece.

With most manufacturing now taking place in developing countries, there has been much debate about North America's competitiveness. On the whole, we haven't done too badly. Western society has stayed relevant, competitive and wealthy in part by climbing the technology ladder and in part by playing a role in the management and marketing of global production. Owning a great deal of the global capital hasn't hurt either. But those 'useful' trades that can be outsourced or marginalized by new technologies are suffering.

But in the event of an apocalypse? It'll be the few who hold real skills that get the final laugh. Not just because they'll be voted into the bomb shelters, but because they might view the accommodations as an improvement.

I See Blurry

My friends think I'm a slob. My wife thinks I'm a slob. Even I'd agree I'm a slob. This makes me a contradiction in terms because I also hate a mess. In fact, I value cleanliness so much that I have never had a long-term relationship with a woman who was not extremely neat and tidy. My ex was fanatical about cleaning. I remember waking up in the middle of the night to the sound of her vacuuming; it was music to my ears.

As an adult, I've always had a cleaning lady but my reputation for disarray has still gotten out. Holidaying with friends and sharing hotel rooms or crashing on their couches when I visited them overseas has provided my chums with many opportunities to learn the truth of the secret I cannot hide.

It is very frustrating to me, because even though I love cleanliness, I just do not seem able to keep things clean.

There is obviously something wrong with the way my brain is wired. Have you heard of Aphasia? It's a medical condition where some brain-damaged people cannot read certain words. It's not that they don't understand these words; they simply cannot see them. There is a blank, an empty space instead of a word.

I have a similar condition in regard to housework. When it comes to keeping my apartment neat and organized, I see things fuzzy, almost blurry, like a movie that is out of focus. This makes my life very difficult because even though I desperately want to be clean, there is always something that I overlook. When I wash a plate, I'll inevitably miss a spot. When I brush my teeth, I'll forget to put the cap back on the toothpaste tube. And no matter how many times you teach me, I still have no idea how to properly make a bed or fold a shirt. This coupled with my attraction to tidy and argumentative women has generally made for a lot of yelling in my life.

Society does not criticize a man for an illness; it doesn't condemn him for having Cancer or Parkinson's disease. Society is even becoming more tolerant of people with mental disorders — it is not the individual's fault if the chemical balances in their brain are asymmetrical. But I am constantly berated for my messiness, which is not my fault as well. I mean that literally, because I grew up in a uniquely messy house. Whether you believe in nature or nurture, you will most certainly agree that I am blameless.

What do I mean by unique?

What do you do when you are at a friend's house — even an acquaintance's house for that matter — and you are standing in the kitchen with a candy wrapper in your hand? You walk over to the sink, open up the cupboard door underneath, and drop the rubbish into that little garbage bin attached to the door. You know the bin is there; because it's on every door in every kitchen you've ever entered.

Except in my childhood home. For some reason, my family did not believe in that garbage bin. In fact, it did not believe in any garbage bin. Garbage bins were blasphemy in the Freedman family home. What we did have was plastic bags. At any time, there would be four or five plastic supermarket bags hanging off chairs and doorknobs in our kitchen. Perhaps my parents thought it was more convenient this way; why walk all the way to the kitchen sink to dispose of your trash when you could just drop it into the bag hanging off the chair you were sitting in? Once a bag was full, it would be transferred to a larger green garbage bag that lay on the floor.

The kitchen bag system illustrates that the problems in our family may have been more organizational in nature than hygienic. We weren't pigs as much as we were slobs. We did have a system — unfortunately there was madness to the method.

Perhaps the best representation of the methodical chaos that was our house was our laundry system. I am referring specifically to the laundry system in house #6. My family had moved five times over the course of my childhood and this last home was a tall split-level. It is crucial to understand the layout of the house if you are to understand the laundry system. There were five floors in all. I lived in the attic. My brother Glen lived on the fourth floor, which had two rooms, and a bathroom which all three boys shared. On the third floor was the family room and a bedroom where my eldest brother David lived. My parents lived in the master bedroom on the second floor, which had an adjoining bathroom. The main floor had a kitchen, a dining room, a living room, a den, a bathroom and a laundry room. Staircases connected all the floors.

I tell you all this because that staircase was of critical importance when it was time to do the laundry. You see, our family did not believe in a conventional laundry system; we believed in teamwork. Let's say I was walking down from my bedroom to the living room to watch some television and I had some dirty underwear and socks. I would kick them down the stairs to the family room on the third floor. Then if David were heading to my parent's bedroom for some reason, he would kick it down another level. Now it only had one level to go. The next person who went down to the kitchen would kick it down to the ground floor. If a pair of underwear or a sock got waylaid on the way, not to worry, someone else would eventually kick it down.

Once the laundry made it to the ground floor, it ran into a bit of a problem, a kind of a bottleneck. The laundry now had to make its way through the kitchen to reach the laundry room. But the only way it would make it to the laundry room is if someone was going there. My family members did not go to the laundry room very often; there was nothing to do there, other than laundry. So more often than not, laundry would just bunch up at the bottom of the stairs at the kitchen entrance. There was a small foyer between the kitchen and the laundry room, so when someone reached maximum frustration over the pile in front of the kitchen, they would viciously hurl it into that foyer. The laundry in that room was usually ankle deep.

Everyone's laundry traveled in this fashion. And just like a snail leaves a trail of sorts as it oozes along its way, our laundry left its own trail, underwear or towels or pantyhose, strewn across our staircase. It was a mild inconvenience. If somebody were vacuuming the carpet — an infrequent occurrence — they would simply vacuum around the laundry.

Every now and then, my mother would go into the foyer and start gathering laundry to wash in massive industrial size loads. A keen admirer of ancient Egyptian construction techniques, she would pile clean and dry laundry on top of the dryer in a giant pyramid formation. We had no use for drawers in our house; if I needed underwear in the morning before I went to school, I would go down to the laundry room and dig through that pyramid. The trick was not to topple it over.

And if something needed to be hang-dried, my family had

the perfect energy-efficient solution. Heat rises, so shirts, pantyhose and other delicates were hung on light fixtures to best capture those warm currents. When someone needed a shirt, they would simply walk up to the appropriate chandelier, take off their shirt, and put the hanger back.

Growing up, nobody in the family seemed particularly bothered by our messy house. As a young boy, I wasn't bothered either, in fact just the opposite. One day, I had a bunch of friends over at the house and we had the most sensational sock fight in the basement. I remember clocking my friend Stewart in the head with a rolled-up hockey sock just as he dived off the stairs into a three-foot-deep pile of dirty clothes. What a great house I had! Who needs snowball fights when you've got a room that is ankle deep in laundry? I could not have been any older than seven at the time.

But as a teenager, my family's messiness caused me great embarrassment. Every now and then, the mess would overcome me and I would work myself into a cleaning frenzy. I would pick up every wayward newspaper, every abandoned peach pit. I would polish the kitchen from top to bottom. I would go through the pantry, organizing shelves, and throwing out expired foods. I would come up with charts and systems, which I would present to my family at dinnertime, on how we might organize ourselves so as to keep our house clean. My family would always smile and nod; but nothing changed.

Living abroad for so long, I tried to make it home at least once a year. I have usually stayed with my parents when I visited. Sometimes, I had a woman with me. Given my girlfriends' proclivities for neatness, I'd warn them well in advance.

One girlfriend of mine, Francesca, insisted on cleaning the kitchen the first time she came home with me. She was good Italian stock. She knew how to clean. Her mother knew how to clean. I was proud of her traditional work ethic. Within minutes of entering my parent's home she was at it, washing pots, organizing cupboards, scrubbing the kitchen floor. After two hours, the kitchen looked brand new, like something out of *Architectural Digest*. She had just finished and was getting a snack out of the fridge when my father walked into the kitchen. I think she was expecting some praise. He looked around and said, "Please be careful not to make a mess." Like son like father; I guess I'm not the only one with a fuzzy and blurry place.

Why God Lets Bad Things Happen

For most of my life, I've questioned the existence of God. I don't identify with people who have blind faith, although I try to respect their beliefs. Where I get irritated though is with people who abandon this faith, just because things don't work out quite the way they had expected.

An old girlfriend, Jennifer, initially seemed no different to me. But one day our conversation turned to religion. In between bites of dim sum, she revealed not only her faith in the God of the bible, but her plan to become more religious. She told me that once she got married she planned to go to synagogue weekly and keep a kosher home. I asked her what she would do if her future husband did not share these beliefs. Her eyes flashed, "I expect anybody I end up with would respect me enough to do the same."

I was taken aback. Not just by her disregard for her

heretofore-undiscovered husband's philosophy (let's hope he remembers to take out the trash), but by her procrastination. If you believe enough in God to follow His arguably draconian laws, then who are you to delay implementation?

But I wasn't going to go there. Instead, I politely asked her why she believed so strongly in God. She told me that when she was a little girl her father had a brain tumor. Surgery was his only option and with that only a 1-in-a-100 chance of survival. He did survive. And given what happened, she's always believed she owes something to God.

But what about the ninety-nine other families who lost their father to that same tumor? They pull out their hair. They curse and cry. Surely there can't be a god if he let their good father die?

The fact is, only 1-in-a-100 were going to survive this disease, and it had to be somebody. Why does everybody bring God into it?

I believed in God when I was a young child. I believed in lots of things then. I believed my parents when they told me that my pet guinea pig, Georgie — who had broken his leg — was given to a farmer. A couple of years later, I learned the truth. It made me question a lot of things.

In the private Jewish school I attended, religious studies were a major part of the curriculum. And while I no longer believed in dead guinea pigs breathing fresh country air or the certainty of a biblical God, I did enjoy the intellectual stimulation of my religious education. I repeatedly asked my teachers why a just and perfect God would do things that to my mind looked just plain mean. My teachers would usually respond that I was simply not capable of understanding the mind of God — that I was to God as an ant was to me. I found the analogy rather patronizing.

But then I saw *The Matrix*, and my teachers' words suddenly made perfect sense. The movie sparked a thought on why a just and perfect god might allow so much suffering to happen.

We've all had nightmares where our loved ones die. I remember having such a dream as an infant: my parents, my brothers, my whole family dead. I remember my sadness, my fear and my hatred of God. This was obviously back when I still believed in God — and Georgie was still alive.

I remember waking up from the dream in a cold sweat. After a few seconds, I realized that everything was OK. Nobody was dead. I was anxious, still angry, but I was also relieved. I did not remain angry with God for long. How could I be mad at him? It was just a dream.

I think of Jennifer's father. I think of the ninety-nine other families who lost their father to that brain tumor. I try to imagine myself in their shoes. I try to imagine worse: a plane crash from which I emerge, horribly disfigured, my entire family dead. I am devastated. I am angry. What kind of God would allow this to happen? I live for many years bitter and alone. And then I die.

But it doesn't end there. I open my eyes. And what do I see? All of my loved loves surrounding me. They are glowing figures of light. And so am I. They are actually laughing, laughing at how upset I was from their deaths. My life on earth was only a small part of the journey; it was no different than a dream. But I am here now, and they are here now, and everything is OK. I am happy. And then I see God. He is looking at me. He has a slight mischievous smile. I'm still a little bit angry, but it's passing. There was a lot more to life than meets the eye.

I think that's what my teachers meant when they called me an ant. I may be an intelligent entity, but that does not mean I know the whole story. I am a three-dimensional entity in a four-dimensional universe. I cannot see all the angles. So if I choose to believe in an all-powerful and all-knowing God, then who am I to judge him?

But something else occurs to me. If God can be forgiven for the fact that our lives are no different than a dream, then perhaps people should be forgiven for losing their faith when they didn't know it was a dream. Until we walk a mile in their shoes, who are we to judge them? And if it's hypocrisy, well, let's just cut them some slack. After all, they are only ants.

Food Poisoning Is Only Fair

I have no sympathy for people who get food poisoning. And yes, I have suffered from it myself — on more than one occasion.

My worst experience was on an international flight to Hong Kong. I had eaten a chicken sandwich just before the flight and about five hours in, I began to feel that all-too-familiar hollow sensation in the belly. You know the feeling. I fought it. "I will not throw up … I will not throw up," I told myself. Then we hit turbulence. This helped convince me that perhaps I would throw up after all. I reached for one of those sick-bags in the pocket in front of me and proceeded to empty my stomach.

This was not one of those fake 'put on your seat belt, please' kinds of turbulence. This was the real deal. The plane was rocking hard enough for the flight attendant to stop what she was doing and sit down. I was in the front row and she was in the crew seat, strapped in, and directly facing me. She was cute and I tried to smile. She looked away.

I sat cradling the bag, enjoying that heavenly moment of relief that one gets in between hurls, when I felt a vicious stirring from a different part of my body. I swear this is true. Turbulence and seat belt signs notwithstanding, I got up, carefully placed the sick-bag on the floor and hurried to the bathroom. The flight attendant made no attempt to stop me.

I won't bore you with the nauseating details of what happened next. Except to say that I was less than pleased when I returned to my seat. You see there is a design flaw with airplane sick bags. They are not so different from the paper bags I used as a child to carry my lunch to school. But unlike those paper bags, I did not fill this one with bananas and tuna fish sandwiches.

I tell you this story simply so we can all agree that I understand food poisoning. I may even qualify as an expert. And yet, I still have no sympathy for those who suffer it. The truth is, I believe I got what was coming to me.

My logic is simple. When I think about the sheer volume of food that is grown, slaughtered, processed, distributed and consumed in any given year, I'm actually pretty impressed that more people do not die from food poisoning, let alone get sick from it. According to the Center for Disease Control, there are 325,000 hospitalizations in the US each year due to food poisoning, with 5,000 fatalities. The majority of incidents stem from complications associated with our reliance on an animal-based diet. Improper food preparation also plays a role.

When watching the *Discovery Channel*, how many of you root for the lion when you see it chasing down a weak and vulnerable gazelle? Do you not agree the occasional bout of indigestion from swallowing too many hooves in one sitting is just desserts?

It's not like we can't do a better job of protecting ourselves. Our priorities are just in the wrong place. Be it food preparation, cleanliness of slaughter facilities or careful use of pesticides, insecticides and antibiotics, a coordinated effort on this front would likely reduce occurrences of food poisoning.

But we are cheap when it comes to food. I say this because recent statistics show America spends only 10 percent of its income on food. This does not seem like a whole lot to me when you compare it with some of the other things people fritter their money away on, like medical care, on which Americans spend 12 percent.

I say 'fritter' because no doubt these horrifyingly high medical costs are inflated by obesity-related illnesses. Statistics show obese people are far more likely to suffer cancer, stroke, heart disease and diabetes in their lifetime. To what extent does obesity inflate medical costs? I don't know the answer to that, but just like portion size at McDonalds, I bet it's not going to be small.

If we started making better decisions about the amount of food we ate and the way we produced and prepared it, I bet we could reduce our medical expenses by far more than the increased cost of food.

Ultimately, I think people are getting exactly what they deserve, particularly when they eat a bad piece of meat. And before you get too irritated with me, remember I'm no vegan. I'm a heavy-duty carnivore myself. I freely admit I don't give a whole lot of thought to food industry practices and the cows that fill my belly. I ignore it all when I sit down to eat — or more accurately — overeat. Thank you, fast metabolism.

But my callous position also reflects my consideration of the moral implications of eating another living creature. The way I see it, in the off chance that there is some karmic debt accruing to mankind, we're not even repaying a fraction of it, what with our tummy aches. It would be one thing if we were eating for survival, but with seven billion people on the planet and one hundred and thirty million people overweight in North America alone, I think we've fulfilled our genetic responsibilities. Haven't we had enough?

A Wicked Itch

It was just after midnight and three of us stood outside the entrance to Wicked, the swingers club in Toronto. Neither Joanna, Kristina or me had ever been in a sex club before.

I've always avoided situations like this. Not that I haven't had an acceptable share of casual encounters, but they've always been on my terms. For me, the perfect one-night stand has been the encounter with the 'good' girl, the one who doesn't normally 'do that sort of thing.' Except for the night that she meets me. That's the night she decides she wants to be 'bad.'

My fear of group encounters is not because I'm a prude. If I trusted everyone's health status, I'd skip through Wicked's front door. But I don't trust it. And there's way too much going on in a place like Wicked for me to feel safe: too many limbs in too many places; too many things that could go wrong.

I bring this up, because I'm a mess of contradictions when it comes to a place like Wicked. Deep down I didn't want to go there. But deep-deep down, I did want to go there. Joanna and Kristina were providing me with an opportunity to enter Wicked on my own terms.

I had no romantic history with either of these women when we first entered the club, and no desire to change that status. We were three friends that in an unusual turn of events — i.e. three bottles of wine — suddenly found ourselves at the front door. We vowed to watch out for each other and ensure nothing undesirable happened. Of course, 'undesirable' means different things to different people.

There are three levels to Wicked. The first floor houses the nightclub, which is like any other hotspot, with drinks, music and dancing. The second and third floors are where the action takes place. You pay a small fee to enter the nightclub. You pay an additional fee to upgrade your membership to access the second and third floor.

We decided to adopt a 'wait-and-see' attitude, and paid only for the first floor. It was a hotbed of activity. There was a long bar on the left, tables on the right and a very crowded dance floor. There was a stage at the back of the room. We climbed onto it and started to dance. Now, I'm no Brad Pitt but I was less than impressed. I did not see a single person that struck me as attractive, more so the opposite. I certainly wasn't feeling any particular urge to bang anyone in this gang.

But we did not stay on the stage for very long. Against the back wall was a door that opened into a stairway. It was partially blocked with empty cardboard boxes. A back-way to the forbidden second-floor swinger's club, perhaps? "Let's check it out," Joanna said. Kristina did not want to go up. She was losing her nerve. So was I, but I was not yet ready to bow out. We tried to convince Kristina, but it was no use. Joanna and I were now on our own.

Joanna and I snuck into the stairway. "Not only are we sex deviants, but we're cheap sex deviants," I thought, as we climbed over the boxes. The door at the top was unlocked. We opened it and emerged onto the second floor. There was no one else up there. We were completely alone.

The second floor of Wicked was essentially a long hall with rooms, partitions and all the expected swinger club accoutrements along the way. At one end was an outside patio and the back-way stairway that we had just used. At the other end was a reception counter and a main staircase that leads down to the nightclub and up to a third floor.

By far, the centerpiece of the club was a large canopied area with multiple beds placed side by side in the shape of a 'U.' This 'Bedouin' tent could easily accommodate twelve people.

I was actually pretty impressed. The place was not opulent, but it was not disgusting either. The sheets covering the mattresses looked clean. I reckoned it was about a seven and a half on the hygiene scale, as good as any $199 per night hotel I've stayed at in New York.

We were standing outside on the patio, wondering where everybody was, when the door banged open and a short, bald man popped out. He looked like the evil genius in the movie *The Princess Bride*; the only difference being our villain was wearing nothing but a towel. Our new friend informed us that we were not allowed to wear our street clothes up here. We had to change. Apparently, membership does have its privileges and sixty dollars would buy us legitimacy via a locker and some towels. We walked over to the reception area and forked over the dough.

Now while I gave Wicked a seven and a half out of ten for cleanliness, I gave the lockers a three out of ten. They were not much bigger than the ubiquitous shoe locker found in most fitness centers. Inside each locker were two threadbare towels — our only cover for the evening. We silently undressed, avoiding eye contact. "Cheap bastards," I muttered, as I stuffed our clothes into the tiny locker.

I then noticed the sign that read 'Only One Towel Per Member.' "No, make that fucking cheap bastards," I added. My one clean towel was worth its weight in gold as far as I was concerned. It had to be protected at all costs.

Joanna suggested we get into the hot tub. Years ago, at the end of a bachelor party, I saw a drained hot tub after a night of debauchery. It looked like a soiled diaper. So, I definitely did not want to get into this tub. But I was trying to loosen up and go with the flow — and we were the first ones there. I got into the murky waters, carefully folding my towel and placing it on the cleanest-looking edge.

Joanna and I sat side-by-side, neck deep in the hot water, peering over the edge of the tub. I felt like a crocodile in some muddy African river as I waited for thirsty zebras to arrive. We did not have to wait long. Swingers were now materializing in full force. Their numbers may have been picking up, but not their looks. Swingers must share a common ancestor with sun-worshiping nudists, who are also known for their poor genetics.

But there's always one exception to every rule. She was walking slowly towards me: a princess among peasants. She was accompanied by a hairy beast of a man. The two of them stopped at the edge of the tub. The princess murmured something, and then dropped her towel and gracefully entered the water. This was followed by a loud splash as her companion lurched in.

'Anastasia' was an eleven out of ten. She was in her early twenties, about five foot seven, with long brown hair and big brown eyes. I call her Anastasia because she looked like the Russian princess of the same name — a human version of the Walt Disney cartoon character. That is, if that same cartoon was sitting on the edge of a hot tub, legs splayed open, and some dude's head in between them.

I don't know if the guy was Russian, or if she was Russian, but in my imagination, they were both Russian. I imagined that he was some evil ex-KGB extortionist while she was a lost descendant of royalty. I imagined that things must have been going very badly for her indeed to choose to be with a man like him. I wished I could help her regain her rightful place on the Russian throne.

Until that moment, Joanna and I had never so much as kissed. We were friends — friends without benefits. I had just moved to Toronto and while I had gone on a lot of dates with a lot of women, I had avoided casual hookups. Dating when you're forty is serious business — biological clocks are ticking and I didn't want to waste anybody's time if I didn't feel a strong connection. I still don't know what her perspective was; when you're single, being friends with a single person of the opposite sex can be complicated.

Given the unique circumstances and the spotlight of another couple, we kissed. The awkward charade did not last long. Within minutes of their arrival, Anastasia and 'Dmitri' got up and left the tub. Without an audience, Joanna and I could stop. "Let's get out of here." Joanna said.

I concurred and suggested a quick shower. I was troubled when she declined, suggesting that we stay with the Russians. My trepidation was only to intensify throughout the evening. I grabbed my clean towel, carefully cradling it in my hands as we followed the Russians back to the Bedouin tent.

The Bedouin tent had a canopy above the beds and short walls and curtains surrounding them, providing a sense of privacy. The diagram on the next page shows the rough layout of the area and its occupants. It was early in the evening, and there were eight people — including Joanna and I — on the mattresses.

Joanna and I were in the corner marked 'X' — only a few feet away from Anastasia and Dmitri. I felt really good about my position. I had a wall to my left and a wall to my back with Joanna on my right. I carefully folded my towel, and placed it in the corner furthest from the action. Joanna and I lay on our sides in classic spoon position as we observed our surroundings.

I am a guy and I wanted to fit in, so Joanna and I were kissing once again – just to fit in. Our hands were fitting in too. Her hands were fitting in twice as much as mine because when I glanced over her shoulder, I noticed one of her hands was on the backside of the Russian dude, who was preoccupied with Anastasia.

"Shit," I thought to myself. "Stay cool. Stay calm. You're a big boy, now. This isn't a big deal. You want to be a porn star? So be a porn star, you fucking weenie!"

I closed my eyes and tried to think porn star thoughts. We continued to kiss. I kept my eyes tightly closed. Don't look! Don't Look! But then curiosity got the better of me. I opened my eyes just a crack and peeked over her shoulder. Oh no! Joanna's hand was now reaching between Dmitri's legs! Bemused by the turn in events, he had lifted his head, and was now looking at me.

It was at this moment that I began to feel deflated — and I do mean this in the literal sense. Now, normally this is something that would cause any red-blooded man great concern, but in this case it was a good thing. That's because I now had a soft but impermeable shield that would protect me from unwanted attention. It would protect me from whatever was to happen next. I started to giggle uncontrollably. "What's so funny?" Joanna asked.

"Nothing. Just keep that fucking hand away from me," I said, pointing at the hand on Dmitri. She let go in embarrassment. I made eye contact with Dmitri again. He looked less than pleased. For the rest of the evening I avoided Joanna's right hand.

In a sudden turn of events, Joanna started to crawl toward Anastasia, who pulled away from Dmitri. The two girls embraced, and without a word spoken, repositioned themselves.

Given this rearrangement, Anastasia's head was now only inches away from my foot. I watched as she kissed Joanna's thigh. Joanna reciprocated in kind. Anastasia then lifted her head, looking straight into my eyes. My body stirred. My head was spinning, screaming that I did not belong there, that I would catch a disease. It was to no avail.

But before my mutinous member could extend an invitation, Anastasia squealed with shock. She looked surprised and uncomfortable. I do not know why. Had Joanna committed a felony at Wicked, a faux-pus perhaps? I do not know. All I know is that the two disentangled, and Joanna returned to my side.

"Now you can keep that fucking mouth away from me, too." I thought but did not say. I was reeling — my brain doing cartwheels in my head.

Joanna suggested I go for a walk and I slunk off. I went to the lounge and sat at the bar. I would have bought a drink except I had no money in my towel. I alternated my eyes between a pornographic video on the television set and an enormous, Indian man giving a massage to his equally enormous partner on top of the massage table.

After about thirty minutes on my own, I headed back to the Bedouin tent. There were perhaps fifteen people on the mattresses now. I inched back to my safe spot, keeping my towel wrapped around me for protection. But where was Joanna? Oh, there she was — in some sort of spider dance with another woman. I watched in bewilderment as the two separated and Joanna crawled not to me, but towards two other women who reminded me of Aesop's disturbing fable, *The Scorpion and the Frog.* If two inverted women equal sixty-nine, then do three inverted women equal 103.5? I do not know. What I did know was that I was starting to feel very sad.

Time passed and eventually Joanna returned to my side. "How are you doing? Do you want to go?" she asked.

My voice was hoarse. "I think I'm ready to leave," I said. "But I don't want to make you leave, not if you're not ready."

"Whatever you want," she said.

"OK. Let's go."

We stood in the locker area, retrieved our crumpled clothes and started getting dressed. The area was crowded, couples coming and going. Joanna was beaming with enthusiasm and forging new friendships. I was forging memories that would haunt my dreams forever: flabby bodies, lank hair and gray teeth. Was everybody ill? Joanna was now talking to a surprisingly healthy-looking black dude, a cross between Will Smith and Bill Cosby. 'Ben' seemed disappointed when we said we were leaving.

Joanna turned to me and said, "You know something. I'm not ready to go. I think I'm going to stay. This is a once in a lifetime opportunity. Let's stay."

"I can't," I whispered. "I'm fucking done."

She started to undress again. Noting that Joanna was back in her towel, Ben turned to me and said, "Are you guys staying?"

"No, I'm going and she's staying." I don't know why I did this, but I offered him my hand and he shook it. I hurried down the stairs.

And as I skipped off into the night, breathing in the clean, fresh air, I felt two conflicting and completely nonsensical emotions. Part of me felt like a seventy-year-old cuckold, who could not satisfy his young wife's enormous libido. But another part of me, a bigger part, felt like a proud papa giving away his daughter on her wedding day. My heart was bursting with happiness that she had found what she was looking for.

But there was a third feeling too, which I noted as I readjusted my pants. Imagination or not, I was feeling one wicked itch.

www.ingramcontent.com/pod-product-compliance
Lightning Source LLC
LaVergne TN
LVHW021452080426
835509LV00018B/2250